Fleet and Crookham Platinum Jubilee Souvenir Programme

Celebrating 70 years of local and national history during the reign of HM Queen Elizabeth II 1952-2022

Compiled by Mark Mabin and designed by Heather Bailey for the Fleet Platinum Jubilee Committee

Milly Marsh

Copyright The Platinum Jubilee Committee

The Contributors Mark Mabin and Heather Bailey asserts the moral right to be identified as the creators of this work

Editing Catherine Stone

Graphic Design Phillipa Bailey

Published 2022 by The Jubilee Committee - An imprint of Translate House
https://www.fleetplatinumjubilee.co.uk/
ISBN: 9781485500124

Printed and bound by Ingram Spark

Every effort has been made to identify copyright holders and obtain their permission for the use of copyright material. Notification of any additions or corrections that should be incorporated in future reprints or editions of this book would be greatly appreciated.

Fleet and Crookham Platinum Jubilee Souvenir Programme

Celebrating 70 years of local and national history during the reign of
HM Queen Elizabeth II 1952-2022

Daisy Smith

Savannah Mapp age 4

This souvenir programme has been compiled by members of the Fleet Platinum Jubilee Committee as a non-profit venture. The programme is being sold at cost, plus an additional £1.00 which is being given to local charities to support the work they do in helping the most disadvantaged in our local community.

Ava McSweeney age 6

This book is a compilation of a Poster Trail that chronicled 70 years of history in Fleet and Crookham, while Queen Elizabeth II has been reigning on the throne of the United Kingdom. It also includes artistic contributions from many local school children, who have designed artworks to celebrate the Queen's Platinum Jubilee and her central role in British life.

The programme includes photographs and an account of the activities that were carried out as part of the Jubilee celebrations between Thursday 2nd June and Sunday 5th June 2022.

It is published as a souvenir of the events associated with celebrating the Queens Platinum Jubilee, and the period of local history throughout which she has reigned.

The Platinum Jubilee Committee would like to acknowledge the help that has been provided by the Fleet and Crookham Local History Group, and particularly Phylis Ralton, in the research and preparation of information contained in the historical aspects of the posters and the provision of illustrative photographs.

Finally, the Platinum Jubilee Committee would also like to thank and acknowledge Aldershot, Farnham and Fleet Camera Club, and local photographer Kevin Whibley of Captured Moment and Nigel Box for the provision of the photographs that were used to chronicle the events of the Platinum Jubilee celebrations.

Winnie Uccelli

Crookham Infant School

Winnie Uccelli (Winner of Infant School Competition)

Heatherside Infant School

Savannah Mapp

Ava McSweeney

All Saints C of E Junior School

Evelyn Samuel

Heatherside Junior School

Freya Henson

Sahana Karthik

Katrina Bhawan

Velmead Junior School

Isla Dobson

Elvetham Heath Primary School

Summer Walsh

Milly Marsh (Winner of Junior School Competition)

Calthorpe Park School

Rebeca Walsh-Esparza

Court Moor School

William Yates

Toby Ricketts

William Sharples

Dexter Dawson

Molly Milton

Matthew Briggs-Humphrey

Edith Jesse

Amelia Raby

Daisy Smith (Overall Winner of Schools Competition)

1952

- **January:** Development of the first effective polio vaccine by Jonas Salk.
- **February:** King George VI died following a prolonged illness. Princess Elizabeth was on a Royal Visit to Kenya when she acceded to the throne.

- **February:** Queen Elizabeth II becomes Monarch of the Commonwealth realms.

- **May:** The first passenger jet flight route opens between London and Johannesburg.
- **July:** Egyptian Revolution under Gamal Abdel Nasser overthrows King Farouk and ends British occupation.
- **November:** The United States successfully detonates the first hydrogen bomb, codenamed "Ivy Mike", at Eniwetok Atoll in the Marshall Islands in the central Pacific Ocean, with a yield of 10.4 megatons.

Map of Fleet as it was in 1950 to demonstrate the growth of the town over the past 70 years.

3rd Fleet Brownies Troop Established

The 3rd Fleet Brownies Troop was established in 1952. They, like the queen will be celebrating, in this jubilee year, 70 years of service to the community.

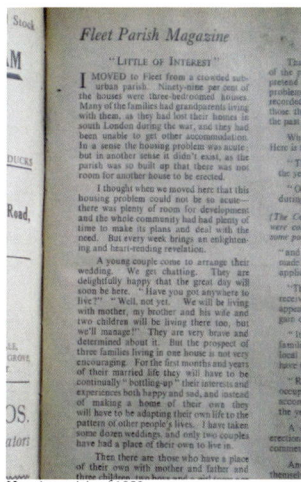

Housing crisis of 1952

Tennis Player John Feaver Born in Fleet

Born in Fleet in February 1952, John achieved success as a doubles player on the tennis circuit, playing in 11 Grand Slams. A career pinnacle was reaching the semi-finals of the 1982 French Open with his partner Cássio Motta, where they lost to the eventual championship winners Sherwood Stewart and Ferdi Taygan.

John's other claim to fame is as a big hitter. For more than 20 years he held the record for serving the most aces in a single match at Wimbledon. Using an old-fashioned wooden racket, 42 winners flew past Australian legend, and three-time champion, John Newcombe in the second round match.

As a member of Great Britain's Davis Cup squad between 1977 and 1983, he played alongside John Lloyd and Buster Mottram. Following his retirement as a player, a career in sport and media saw John becoming a Lawn Tennis Association tournament director. He's also been a great supporter of the charity StreetGames, which seeks to "transform communities through the power of sport."

Fleet cycle speedway 1952.

1953

- January: Dwight D. Eisenhower is inaugurated as President of the United States.
- March: The Queen's grandmother, Queen Mary, dies aged 85
- June: The Coronation took place in Westminster Abbey on 2 June 1953.
- February: Release date of Disney's

Peter Pan.
- March: Death of Stalin.
- April: James Watson and Francis Crick publish their discovery of the structure of DNA.
- May: First ascent of Mount Everest's summit, by Sir Edmund Hilary and Sherpa Tenzing Norgay.
- July: End of the Korean War.
- November: Independence of Cambodia from France.
- December: The first colour television is produced. The first broadcast colour TV programme was on Jan 1 1954.

Fleet Celebrates the Coronation

Coronation year was celebrated in style with 12 days of events including a sports gymkhana and King and Queen. There were two carnival processions, the King starting at the station and the Queen at Crookham, both meeting at the Oatsheaf before touring the district. It was an unforgettable period for the children. The one-off special carnivals stirred interest in establishing an annual event, which commenced in 1956 and has been run since, stopped only by Covid in 2020 and 2021.

Major Renovations at Fleet Town Football Club

The club, which has a 250-seat stand, moved to its home ground at Calthorpe Park in March 1923 when Lord Calthorpe of Elvetham Hall made the site available. In 1953 the existing pitch, pavillion and floodlighting were originally installed. The club's best performance in the FA Cup came in 2007–08 and 2008–09, when it reached the third qualifying round.

Gus the Cartoonist Moves to Fleet

Famous resident George William Smith (GUS), famous for his cartoons during the 1950-60s in Punch, Lilliput, The Evening News and Men Only, bought a home on Fitzroy road.

1954

- **April: The song Rock Around the Clock, by Bill Haley and His Comets, brings rock and roll to the American mainstream.**
- **May: The Supreme Court of the United States decides Brown v. Board of Education, ordering an end to racial segregation in public schools.**
- **July: J. R. R. Tolkien publishes The Fellowship of the Ring, the first volume of The Lord of the Rings.**
- **September: The Soviet Union generates first electricity by nuclear power.**
- **May: Roger Bannister breaks the four-minute mile with a time of 3:59.4.**

Fleet Cycle Speedway Team 1954

Church Crookham Garden Society Formed

The Ryelaw Garden Society was founded in 1954 by residents of Ryelaw Road as an outlet for their interest in gardening. At some time in its early era, the Society began trading garden supplies, and until 1997 traded from sheds located in Moore Close.

The name of the Society was changed to Church Crookham Garden Society to reflect the wider residential locations of its members. Shows were organised, and now two shows per year are run, one in the spring and one in late summer. In 1997 the ground occupied by the Society's sheds was subject to planning consent for residential building and the Society moved to a purpose-built concrete garage located in the car park of the Crookham Memorial Hall in Sandy Lane, Church Crookham.

First Parish Pantomime

Fleet Parish Church began the tradition of an annual pantomime in 1954 with the production of Babes in the Wood, and has staged a pantomime every year since.

Peter Driver Wins Gold at British Empire and Commonwealth Games

Aged 22, runner Peter Driver won the six-mile distance in a time of 29:09.4, which was a Commonwealth Games record and the first time an athlete had run the distance in under 30 minutes. Peter was a member of South London Harriers at the time, but later became club secretary of Fleet and Crookham Athletic Club in 1961.

1955

- April: Winston Churchill resigns as prime minister due to his failing health.
- April: The Salk polio vaccine, having passed large-scale trials earlier in the United States, receives full approval by the Food and Drug Administration.
- April: Death of Albert Einstein.
- April: Anthony Eden becomes Prime Minister.
- September: Commercial television starts with the first ITV broadcast.
- September: Death of James Dean, American actor.
- October: Princess Margaret calls off her plans to marry Group Captain Peter Townsend.
- November: Antimatter first produced.

Stevens Bros, Fleet

Mr Stevens, a Crookham smith, opened a second smithy and coach building business in Fleet Road. The premises extended through to Albert Street. His six sons were each apprenticed to a different related trade and the business logically progressed to horseless carriages. It became a thriving car sale and repair business and later petrol pumps were added.

Aircraft Crash Occurs at Frank Pullens' Stable

Frank Pullen, a wealthy businessman and racehorse owner, was the founder of Pullen Estates which grew into one of South London's leading developers. Pullen went onto become a leading race horse owner with stables most famously at Josh Gifford's yard in Findon, Sussex. In 1955 he had stables in Fleet which were heavily damaged when a jet aircraft crashed on the site between Dinorben Avenue and the Basingstoke Canal. The aircraft landed at the rear of the stable, spraying burning jet fuel over the buildings.

None of Pullen's horses were killed, but all were so shaken up that the national hunt season was ruined for his stable.

The pilot of the aircraft ejected, but there was insufficient height for the full cycle of his ejection of the seat to occur before it struck a tree, killing the unlucky man.

Princess Margaret had just taken her seat in the Royal Enclosure at the Royal Aircraft Establishment and witnessed the mushroom of smoke as the aircraft hit the ground. She was reported to have been greatly disturbed by the incident.

1956

- January: Independence of Sudan from Britain.
- March: Full independence of Pakistan.
- September: The Duke of Edinburgh's Award (commonly abbreviated to DofE) is a youth awards programme founded in the United Kingdom in 1956 by Prince Philip, Duke of Edinburgh, that has since expanded to 144 nations. The awards recognise adolescents and young adults for completing a se-

ries of self-improvement exercises modelled on Kurt Hahn's solutions to his "Six Declines of Modern Youth".

- November: The Hungarian Uprising is crushed by Soviet troops.
- October: Egyptian President Nasser's nationalisation of the Suez Canal triggers the Suez crisis.
- October: Britain opens its first nuclear power station, Calder Hall.

First Fleet Carnival

The Chamber of Trade called a meeting in response to the recognised need for a public hall. They decided that £10,000 should be raised by holding an annual carnival; the first being held in 1956.

Freddie Mills at the Carnival

First Fleet Carnival Queen

The first of the modern-day carnivals was held in the summer of 1956 on the Firs Meadow in Crookham Road, where the police station used to stand. The special guest was the world light heavyweight boxing champion, Freddie Mills, and the first carnival queen was Judy Poulter. The event was a great success, inspiring strong community spirit and participation.

Crookham War Memorial Hall Errected

Crookham Memorial Hall was erected in 1956 as a living and active memorial to those who lost their lives in the Second World War. This hall added to the existing Willis Hall on the site, that commemorated those who lost their lives in the First World War.

The Queen Mother Visits the Troops at Queen Elizabeth Barracks Crookham

Queen Elizabeth the Queen Mother, Colonel-in-Chief of the Royal Army Medical Corps, visited the depot and training establishment at Crookham on 13 July 1956.

1957

- January: Harold Macmillan becomes Prime Minister.
- March: Independence of Ghana from Britain.
- March: Treaty of Rome, which would eventually lead to the European Union.
- July: Altea Gibson becomes the first African American tennis player to win Wimbledon.

- August: Independence of the Federation of Malaya.
- October: Launch of Russian Sputnik 1 and the beginning of the Space Age.

- December: First flight of the Boeing 707.

1957 - NGTE Test Cells 1 and 2 commissioned - used to test high altitude jet engines

Frank Whittle and his team of engineers were the recognised inventors of the jet engine. Following the end of the war, development of the jet engine continued with recognised strategic importance. In 1946 Whittle's company Power Jets Ltd, based at Pyestock, was nationalised and renamed the National Gas Turbine Establishment, becoming part of the Ministry of Supply. By this time, Frank Whittle and his lead designers had resigned.

Two years later, the whole facility was moved to Pyestock, Farnborough, adjacent to the RAE wind tunnels. The National Gas Turbine Establishment (NGTE) Pyestock site was extended to accommodate this move and 195 acres of surplus land was acquired from the War Office. The significant task of constructing the test facilities started during the 1950's. In 1952, the Battle Test House was commissioned and marked the NGTE's foray into testing naval based gas turbines. New research facilities Test Cell 1 & 2 were constructed, that were to be the first high altitude jet engine test beds in the country. The construction took three years to complete and the cells were commissioned in 1957. By this time, the large compressors and test beds had been commissioned in the Battle Test House, with power being provided from a new steam generating boiler.

Fleet Cinema Closes

Fleet's cinema was located at 287 Fleet Road, on the site of the former 357-seat, King George V Cinema, which had operated from 1918 to 1937, before being demolished by the County Cinemas Chain. Originally called the County Cinema, it had seating for 610 in the stalls and 164 in the circle. In 1939 it was taken over by the Oscar Deutsch chain of Odeon Theatres Ltd.
In 1946 it was renamed the Odeon. It was closed on 12th October 1957, the building was demolished, and shops and a Co-Op-

1958

- July: First parking meters installed in the UK.
- July: NASA formed.

- July: Prince Charles is given the title "The Prince of Wales".
- August: Notting Hill race riots in London.
- October: Sovereignty of Christmas Island is transferred from the United Kingdom to Australia.

- October: First broadcast of the long-running BBC Television children's programme Blue Peter.
- December: The British motorway system opens with the M6 Preston bypass.

Fleet, Crookham and Crondall Girl Guides

Fleet & Church Crookham and Crondall Girl Guiders become a District and part of Aldershot Division. Lady Olave-Baden Powell, the wife of the founder of Scouting, Lord Robert Baden-Powell, visited Fleet to attend and address a local fete.

Tweseldown - World Pentathlon Riding Event and New Control Tower

Tweseldown has a rich and varied history of equine and military use stretching back over 160 years. The course has held Military Reviews for the Queen, hosted Olympic events, National hunt, point to point, the world Pentathlon riding events and is now staging regular British Eventing and Unaffiliated Horse Trials and cross-country schooling sessions.

Racing began at Tweseldown in 1866 and was staged for the benefit of officers from Aldershot Garrison. The Grand Military Gold Cup was run on the Hampshire course until it was moved to Sandown in 1887 but National Hunt meetings continued to be organised at Tweseldown until 1932. At one time as many as seven fixtures took place annually.

Tweseldown hosted the Eventing for the 1948 Olympic Games, the 1958 World Pentathlon Riding event and staged the first Sunday race meeting with legal betting in 1996.

Holy Trinity Catholic Church Parish formed

The Church Crookham Parish of The Holy Trinity was formed in 1958 by a division of the parish of Fleet. There was a church in the area already, the Garrison Church of Our Lady of Lourdes. This church, which had been built for the troops about 1920, had been looked after by the Salesian Priests from Farnborough who acted as Officiating Chaplains. This duty was taken over by the Parish Priest. The territory of the new parish comprised the area of Fleet south of the Basingstoke Canal and the villages of Crookham, Dogmersfield, Winchfield, Ewshot and Crondall. Daily Mass began in 1958 when the first Parish Priest took up residence in the presbytery in Moore Road.

In 1960 a plot of land in Aldershot Road was purchased. On this site an old thatched house called Woodey Corner had stood. One day the owner Captain Duckworth and his wife went out, leaving a fire in one of the rooms. When they returned, the house was completely burnt down.

The growth of the parish and the running down of the army necessitated the building of a new church. This was designed and constructed by the same company that built the Fleet Catholic Church and the design closely resembles it. The church was opened in 1968, and the following year the presbytery was built and the old presbytery in Moore Road was sold.

1959

- **WORLD POPULATION REACHES THREE BILLION.**
- **January: Cuban Revolution ends.**
- **February: Rock and roll musicians Ritchie Valens, Buddy Holly and The Big Bopper die in a plane crash.**
- **February: Independence of Cyprus.**
- **March: Uprising in Tibet against China leads to the exile of the Dalai Lama.**
- **October: The U.S.S.R. probe Luna 3 sends back the first ever photos of the far side of the Moon.**
- **November: Beginning of the Vietnam War, which lasted for almost twenty years until 1975.**

- **November: The Oscar-winning film Ben-Hur premieres.**
- **December: Great Chinese Famine begins in China.**
- **December: First documented AIDS case.**

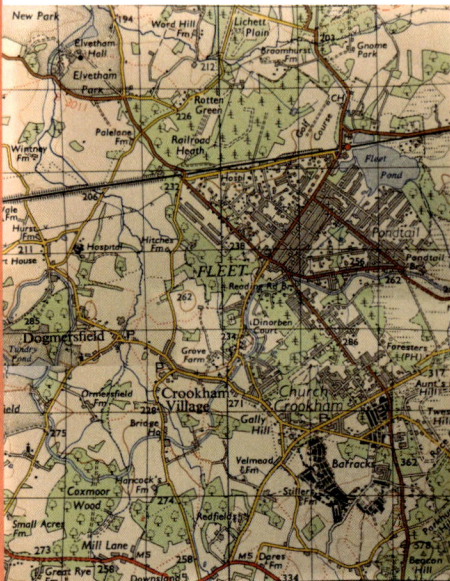

1959 Ordinance Survey Map of Fleet and Crookham

North Hants Tyres

North Hants Tyre and Remoulding Co Ltd. Pictured below is a display stand which was mounted in the marquee of the Fleet Carnival Trade Fair. Stan Burton, the sales manager, is pictured.

Eventually as remoulds became more complex as the speed of cars increased, the company became agents for foreign tyres and wheels. The business moved along the Fleet Road to the junction of Avondale Road.

Crookham Street Social Club in 1909.

The Club was built in Crookham Street and stands 100 yards from the Spice Merchant. Most of the funding to build the club came from local benefactors. In 1959, with the relaxing of betting laws, the club was able to install fruit machines, the proceeds of which funded the addition of a two-storey extension to the side.

1960

- **January:** First crewed descent to the deepest point on Earth, the Mariana Trench.
- **February:** The Queen's third child, Prince Andrew, was born at Buck-

ingham Palace.
- **March:** The Sharpeville Massacre - police opened fire on a crowd in the South African township, resulting in 69 deaths and 180 injuries.
- **May:** Princess Margaret married Antony Armstrong-Jones at Westminster Abbey.
- **May:** European Free Trade Association formed.
- **May:** U-2 incident sparks deterioration in relations between superpowers.
- **May:** The birth control pill becomes commercially available.
- **May:** Construction of the first laser.
- **August:** The Beatles form in Liverpool.
- **September:** American boxer Muhammad Ali wins gold at the Olympics.
- **September:** The first edition of the Summer Paralympic Games is hosted in Rome.

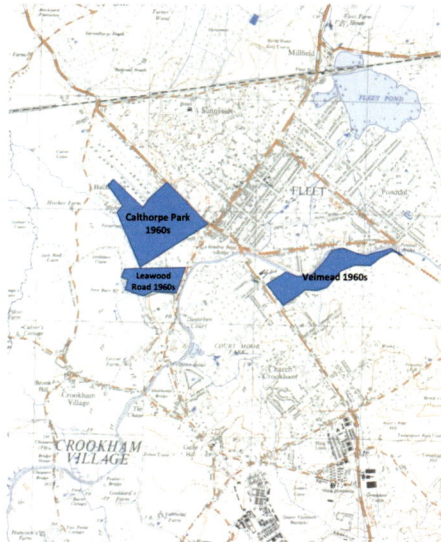

Fleet Map: To demonstrate growth of Fleet over past 70 years. Shaded blue area indicates growth in the 1960s.

Queen Elizabeth II and the Prime Ministers of the Commonwealth Nations, at Windsor Castle.

The Good Old Days!

In 1960 seatbelts were not a legal requirement for adults. But some caring parents could already see the benifit of securing their loved ones into baby car seats. Do you think it made much difference?

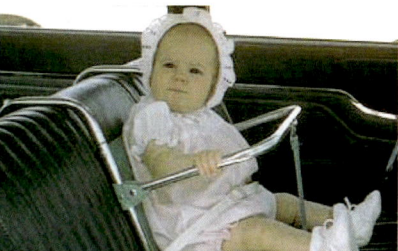

Fleet and Crookham Athletic Club Established

Fleet & Crookham AC was founded in 1960 by a group of enthusiastic individuals, including Malcolm Steggles (a Major in the Parachute Regiment) and Dr. Dave Fearn. Peter Driver also became actively involved after moving into the area in 1961, and represented the club until his untimely death in 1971.

Court Moor School Opens

Fleet Secondary Modern School, the earliest secondary school in the town, moved onto it's current site in 1960 and reopened as Court Moor School on 11 May. At the time, the school had only one building, 500 students and 20 teachers. Court Moor became a comprehensive school in 1974 and is part of the Hart school district.

1961

- **January:** John F. Kennedy is inaugurated as President of the United States.

- **April:** Yuri Gagarin, flying the Vostok 1 spacecraft as part of the Vostok program, becomes the first human in space.
- **May:** In an address to Congress, John F. Kennedy declares the United States' objective of "landing a man on the Moon and returning him safely to the Earth" by the end of the decade. This would be in fact achieved by the Apollo Project, despite several challenges and much doubt.
- **July:** Birth of Diana, Princess of Wales.
- **August:** Construction of the Berlin Wall.
- **December :** The Great Leap Forward ends in China after the deaths of roughly 20-45 million people.

Fleet Rotary Club

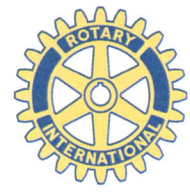

Rotary International is a charity committed to providing service to others, promoting integrity, and advancing an understanding of goodwill and peace through an active fellowship of business, professional, and community leaders. The vision of Rotary is to build a world where people unite and take action to create lasting change indivudally, in communities, and across the globe. Rotary has been running worldwide for 110 years. The Fleet club was established in 1961.

Aircraft crash lands at Tweseldown

On 13th October a Hawker Hunter F4 ETPS crashed into the racecourse at Tweseldown. The cause of the crash was the failure of its fuel pumps while on approach to Farnborough. The pilot ejected successfully at 400 feet and the aircraft crash-landed virtually intact on the nearby Tweseldown racecourse.

The aircraft was recovered back to Farnborough for accident investigation. It was later donated to Cove Air Training Squadron in the 1990s and subsequently sent for scrap. However, the cockpit section was retained at Farnborough for many years for escape procedures training and was also believed to have been used in the Environmental Test cell. It was later rescued by a collector at Boscombe Down, where it is on display at the museum.

Tweseldown has been the site of two aircraft crashes. The earlier crash happened in November 1959, resulting in two fatalities.

Formation of Fleet Townswomen's Guild

Fleet Townswomen's Guild began in the early 60's. This picture is the faithful ladies serving on the hot dog stand at the Carnival. The Townswomen's Guild (TG) is a British women's organisation. There are currently about 30,000 members, belonging to 706 branches and 77 Federations throughout England, Scotland, Wales and Northern Ireland, the Isle of Man and the Isle of Wight.

The Townswomen's Guild is the second largest British women's organisation. It consists of local branches, known as guilds, and federations, which are groups of local guilds who work together throughout the UK.

The movement was formed in 1929, at the instigation of Margery Corbett Ashby and Eva Hubback, when all women over 21 won the right to vote, with the aim of "educating women about good citizenship".

1962

- **July: The Rolling Stones make their debut at London's Marquee Club.**

- **July: World's first regular hovercraft service introduced.**
- **August: Death of Marilyn Monroe.**

- **October: The Second Vatican Council is opened by Pope John XXIII.**
- **October: The Cuban Missile Crisis nearly causes nuclear war.**

Interesting Fact

Fleet had the highest national birthrate in 1962. It is therefore unsurprising that Fleet needed more infant, junior and senior schools, culminating in Calthorpe Park School, which opened in 1969.

Sea Scouts Group Formed

Sea Scout group 26th Odiham formed in Fleet. Sea Scouts are a part of the Scout movement, having a particular emphasis on boating and other water-based activities on the sea, rivers or lakes like canoeing, rafting, scuba, sailboarding.

Sea Scouts provide a chance to sail, learn navigation and engine repair. and compete in regattas. Sea Scouts often have distinctive uniforms.

Ray Oldham becomes Scout Master

Ray Oldham, known as Skip, became the scoutmaster of 22nd Odiham scout troop. Ray has faithfully served as Scoutmaster of 22nd Odiham for 60 years and is a familiar face in and around Fleet. His daughter recently commented that there have been very few occasions when her family have been out in Fleet when an old scout or an old scout's parent doesn't stop Ray for a chat. Ray has scouted with multiple generations of scouts including fathers and sons, and of course now including daughters. Throughout Ray's tenure as Scoutmaster his wife Pat has faithfully served by his side and in her own right as "Akela" of the cub pack. Pat passed away in early 2022 but her legacy lives on the lives of youngsters impacted by her and Ray since the early 60's.

1963

- January: Indonesia-Malaysia confrontation begins.
- March: The Beatles' first record, Please Please Me.
- March: The first report of the Beeching cuts - a railway restructuring plan - was published, The Reshaping of British Railways.
- July: Launch of the first geostationary satellite, Syncom 2.
- August: Martin Luther King Jr. delivers "I Have a Dream" speech at the March on Washington for Jobs and Freedom.
- October: Alec Douglas-Home becomes Prime Minister but lasts only 363 days.
- November: Assassination of John F. Kennedy. Vice President Lyndon B. Johnson assumes office as President of the United States.
- December: Independence of Kenya and Zanzibar and the creation of Malaysia.

Calthorpe Park Scout Hut Opened

9th October 1963 a "new" palatial scout hut was opened at Calthorpe Park, initially home to the 22nd Odiham Scout Troop. It was actually an old military hut moved to the site and opened by Rear Admiral Lawder.

County Commercial Tractor crosses Channel

County Commercial Cars were a major employer throughout Fleet in the 50s, 60s, 70s and 80s. They were particularly known for their 4-wheel drive vehicles, generally tractors. Nearly all of County's tractors were based on Ford tractors. They were very popular in the UK and abroad. They are still prized by collectors and enthusiasts. Perhaps the most unusual of County's tractors was the Sea Horse, which was an amphibious verssion of the County Super-4. It earned a place in the Guinness Book of Records when it was driven across the English channel in 1963, from Cap Griz Nez to Kingsdown, a distance of 28 nautical miles.

Mummers Theatre Group begins staging its traditional Christmas Play.

The Crookham event began in the 1880s and ran until World War II. Public performances were revived in the 1960s. Mummers performances can be caught at the Exchequer, The Spice Merchant, The Green in Crookham Village and the Queens Head in Dogmersfield. They are always performed on Boxing Day. The play is a cross between street theatre and pantomime - it revolves around King George, England's champion, challenging and defeating various opponents in a series of sword fights. The fights have been described as "full blooded" and the wooden swords are usually broken in each fight. With four or more fights per stop and four stops to perform at, that can add up to a lot of broken swords. Although there is a basic script, each year the Mummers add in topical jokes and adlibs. Heckles from the audience are encouraged.

Mumming never really caught on in the rest of the world and is pretty much confined to England. The Crookham Mummers are one of the few teams that have kept going through thick and thin. In the old days it was a vital source of income for some families, but these days donations go to charity.

1964

- **February:** The Beatles' first visit to the United States.
- **March:** Prince Edward, the Queen's fourth child, was born.
- **July:** Civil Rights Act abolishes segregation in the USA.
- **July:** Rhodesian Bush War begins.
- **July:** Independence of Malawi from Britain.
- **August:** The Gulf of Tonkin incident led to the escalation of U.S. military involvement in the Vietnam War.
- **September:** Independence of Malta from Britain.
- **October:** Leonid Brezhnev ousts Khrushchev and assumes power in the Soviet Union.
- **October:** Harold Wilson becomes Prime Minister.

St. Philip and St. James Church in Kings Road Demolished

The corrugated temporary structure for St. Philip and St. James Church in Kings Road Fleet was demolished in 1964 to make way for the building that now stands on the site.

Astronaught Al Worden Lived in Crookham Village

US astronaught Al Worden is the only resident of the area that has ever visited the moon. He lived in the village while training at the Empire Test Pilot School at nearby Farnborough. He went on to serve as the Command Module pilot for the Apollo 15 mission.

Fleet High Street

1965

- **January: Death of Sir Winston Churchill.**

- **February: Death of Malcolm X.**
- **May: First State Visit to West Germany. The Queen's 10-day visit to the Federal Republic of Germany (or West Germany) was the first official visit there by a British royal since 1913. Her visit marked the 20-year anniversary of the end of World War II, helping to symbolise the reconciliation between the two countries.**

- **August: Singapore gains independence.**
- **August: Second Indo-Pakistani War.**
- **November: The death penalty is abolished officially.**
- **December: Second Vatican Council is closed by Pope Paul VI.**

Crookham Junior School Opens

Expansion of Crookham infants, which opened in 1843, took place in 1965 to include a Junior school. The Junior school moved to its current location in Tweseldown Road in recent times.

Clarence Road Baptist Church Opened

The stone laying ceremony for the Baptist Church in Clarence Road was conducted on 26th September 1964, by the Rev George Cumming of Eastbourne. The construction was completed in June 1965 when the building was opened by the minister's wife Enid Shaddick. This was the fourth Baptist Church in Fleet. The first was opened in 1846. Fleet Baptist Church is the oldest established Church in Fleet. Within the walls of the Church are two stones from the original Churchs dated 1849 and the 1892 Church that was demolished in 1970.

1965 - NGTE Test Cell 4 developed for the testing of Concorde

In 1961, the largest testing facility in Europe, Cell 3, was commissioned. This chamber

provided a much more enhanced high altitude testing facility and to provide the enormous volumes of air to the cell, the Air House was built. This contained four large air compressors and exhausters, the number was soon after increased to eight. In order to address the complex problems surrounding the high altitude flight of Concorde, Test Cell 4 was constructed in 1965. This facility allowed for the simulation of supersonic flow conditions for high altitude height and proved invaluable when testing the new Concorde Olympus 593 engine and intakes. The final test cell to be built, Cell 3 West, was the largest altitude chamber and was used to test 50,000lb thrust class turbofan engines. It also allowed engines to be tested in icing conditions. The construction of Cell 3 West and Cell 4 required the construction of two new exhausters. In 1971, an anechoic chamber is consructed on the site, which led to the Queens Award for Enterprise being awarded to the Pyestock site. By 1973, the site was at its largest extent and employed close to 1600 people.

1966

- January: Action Man toy is released.
- March: Theft of football Jules Rimet trophy (World Cup) whilst in London.
- May: The Beach Boys release Pet Sounds.
- May: China's Cultural Revolution begins.
- July: England wins World Cup.
- September: Independence of Botswana.
- October: Independence of Lesotho.
- October: The Aberfan disaster, the catastrophic collapse of a colliery spoil tip (pile of waste coal mining material) in Aberfan, Wales results in 144 deaths.

- November: Independence of Barbados.
- December: Death of Walt Disney.

Wiggs Pool Open

Hilary Wigg built and opened an indoor swimming pool in her back garden in 1966. This was opened to various Fleet groups in 1967 and became the default pool for Fleet's school children and youth clubs to use when teaching children to swim during the late 60s and early 70s.

When Fleet built its own swimming pool in the original sports centre located next to Calthorpe School, it was named the "Hilary Wigg" pool, in honour of the Wigg family's service to the community of Fleet.

Establishment of Fleet Language Circle

Fleet Language Circle was established in 1966 after Colonel Roots, a retired army colonel and linguist, called a meeting at the Lismoyne Hotel in Fleet.

He obviously attracted an enthusiastic group who wanted the opportunity to practise speaking French, German, Italian or Spanish, as 56 years later the club still meets and is thriving. The language circle is currently meeting at the Baptist Church in Basingbourne Road.

The actress Juliet Aubrey was born in Fleet in 1966.

The 60's were obviously a peak time for actresses from Fleet. Juliet Aubrey was born in December 1966. In her career she has gone on to win success and a Bafta in Middlemarch (1994), The Mayor Casterbridge (2003), The Constant Gardener (2005), Midsomer Murders (2006) and most recently Professor T (2021). Juliet is the daughter of local Fleet GP Dr. Aubrey, formerley of Fleet Medical Centre.

Mark Hicks makes Guinness Book of Records

Mr. Mark Hicks of Crookham Village is believed to have had the longest working career in one job in Britain. He started at the age of 10 with the Basingstoke Canal Co., and was still working as a bailiff of the canal four days before

he died 82 years later in July 1966. The Hicks family still occupy the same cottage on the Basingstoke Canal.

1967

- **March:** The Queen Elizabeth Hall is open as a concert venue.

- **May:** The Beatles release their landmark album Sgt. Pepper's Lonely Hearts Club Band.
- **Mid-year:** Summer of Love, in which as many as 100,000 people, mostly young people sporting hippie fashions of dress and behavior, converged in San Francisco's neighbor-

hood of Haight-Ashbury.

- **June:** The Six-Day War, a conflict between Israel and Arab states that resulted in Israel occupying the Gaza Strip, the Sinal Peninsula, the West Bank and the Golan Heights.
- **July:** The Sexual Offences Act 1967 legalises homosexuality between men over 21.
- **October:** The Abortion Act 1967 is passed, legalising abortion on certain grounds.

Fleet Lido Closed

Fleet Lido, located at the Fleet Country Club, fell into disuse after the opening of the new indoor heated Wiggs pool, finally closing in 1967.

Church Crookham Players Established

Church Crookham Players is an amateur drama group serving Church Crookham and Fleet. The group started in 1967 when Christ Church arranged for its congregation to stage a Passion Play around Easter time. The play had been written by the Vicar and many of the actors enjoyed it so much they started to put on plays and monologues. The group developed as Christ Church Players with the Vicar as President and later changed its name to Church Crookham Players to reflect its change to producing secular plays. The group stages two main performances per year in May and November, together with more impromptu productions.

Introduction of Scouts and Guides Church Parades

Anyone who was a scout or guide in Fleet after 1967 will remember the Church Parades that you were expected to attend every threee months. In October 1966, all the Scout and Girl Guide leaders in Fleet had a meeting with the Rev. Colin Deedes. Arising from this the Guide and Scout troops agreed to meet together for quarterly services at the various Churches in Fleet. The first service was held in 1967 at All Saints Church, followed by the congregations of St. Philip and St. James, The Baptist Church, and the Salvation Army Citadel. These special services continue to the present day and have resulted in many different forms of worship as well as building links between cubs and brownie packs, scout troops and guide companies throughout Fleet. The scouts and other uniformed youth organisations play an important part in the annual rememberance day parades.

Eriva Dene Private School

Eriva Dene School was located at 17 Kent Road in Fleet in the private house of its principal Mr Eric Maurice Stevens. The school was a private school offering tuition to boys aged 4-12 years and girls aged 4-15 years. The school opened in 1923. Mr Stevens and his wife Eva, created the name Eriva by combining their first names. Mr. Stevens was also involved in property dealing. The school closed in 1972 with 50 pupils. Mr Stevens continued to live at the propery until he passsed away in March 1983.

1968

- **January:** Prague Spring crushed by the Eastern Bloc military intervention.

- **March:** First performance of an Andrew Lloyd Webber-Tim Rice musical, Joseph and the Amazing Technicolor Dreamcoat.

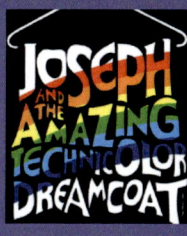

- **April:** Assassination of Martin Luther King Jr. during the Poor People's Campaign.
- **June:** Assassination of Robert F. Kennedy during the Poor People's Campaign.
- **October:** Black Panthers protest on the podium at Mexico Olympics.

- **October:** The Troubles begin in Northern Ireland.
- **November:** Star Trek airs first television's inter-racial kiss.

- **December:** Apollo 8 mission orbits the moon.

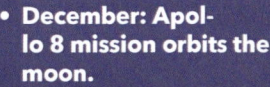

Weslyan Church

Branksomewood Road Fleet, c 1900. The first Wesleyan Methosdist Church was erected in 1887 on a site at the junction of Branksomewood Road and Fleet Road. In 1899 it had become too small and a large brick and stone church, shown here was built on the same site facing Fleet Road. It

was demolished in the late 1960's when a new Methodist church was built in Reading Road South.

The actress Raquel Cassidy was born in Fleet in 1968.

Raquel Cassidy, the actress was born in 1968. She has gone on to win awards for acting and become a regular face on TV with credits that include Downton Abbey (TV and Film), Teachers, Lead Balloon, The Good Karma Hospital. She kindly was the guest to re-open Phyllis Tuckwell in Fleet in 2014.

Fleet Police Station moves to Crookham Road

The original Fleet Police Station was based in Reading Road South and is today used as residential accommodation – that station was closed in 1968. The Service then moved to the purpose built building in Crookham Road. This was built in 1967 and many officers moved there in 1968. The Crookham Road building was put up for sale in 2011 and is currently being redeveloped into housing. Prior to being the police station the site was the location of Fleet's cycle speedway.

County Commercial Specialise in 4-Wheel Drive Tractors

By 1968 County Commercial's business had developed in such a way that the bulk of their business was in 4-wheel drive tractors built around conversion of Ford tractor products.

1969

- **January:** Richard Nixon is inaugurated as President of the United States.
- **March:** Concorde, the world's first supersonic airliner, makes its maiden flight.
- **July:** Prince Charles, first in line to the throne, has his investiture at Caernarvon and becomes the Prince of Wales.

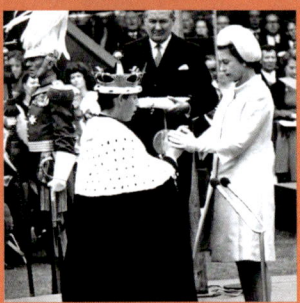

- **July:** Neil Armstrong and Buzz Aldrin become the first two humans on the moon.

- **August:** The Woodstock festival in Bethel, New York, attracts an audience of more than 400,000.
- **Setember:** Muammar Gaddafi overthrows King Idris of Libya in a coup d'état and establishes the Libyan Arab Republic.
- **October:** Creation of Advanced Research Projects Agency Network (ARPANET), the earliest incarnation of the Internet.

All Saints C of E Junior School Opened

All Saints School was built in 1969 and pupils from Heatherside were moved to the school from age 7. Mr. Taylor was the first headmaster.

Heatherside Junior School Built on site of Heatherside Secondary Modern

Heatherside Secondary Modern School was built in 1947, on the site originally occupied by Heatherside House (pictured below) to take the older pupils from the existing Fleet School in Albert Street. It educated children up to the age of 16 until Courtmoor was built and became the Secondary Modern School for the town in 1960. From 1960 the school transitioned into Heatherside Junior School. In 1969 the existing junior school was demolished to be replaced with the current Heatherside junior school building on the same site. Heatherside infants was added to the site in 1980.

Refurbishments at Fleet Station

The Edwardian built Fleet Station was replaced with a flat-roofed new building.

Wyvern Pub 1969

1970

- **January: Maiden flight of the Boeing 747.**
- **January: Containerisation adopted globally, massively boosting global trade.**
- **March: Ratification of the Treaty on the Non-Proliferation of Nuclear Weapons.**
- **April: First 'walkabout'. During a royal tour of Australia and New Zealand, Queen Elizabeth rebelled against centuries of royal tradition when she took a casual stroll to greet crowds of people in person. A 'walkabout' is now a regular practice for British royals.**

- **April: Break-up of the Beatles.**
- **June: Edward Heath becomes Prime Minister.**
- **October: Anwar Sadat becomes President of Egypt.**
- **November: The Bhola Cyclone kills 500,000 people in East Pakistan.**

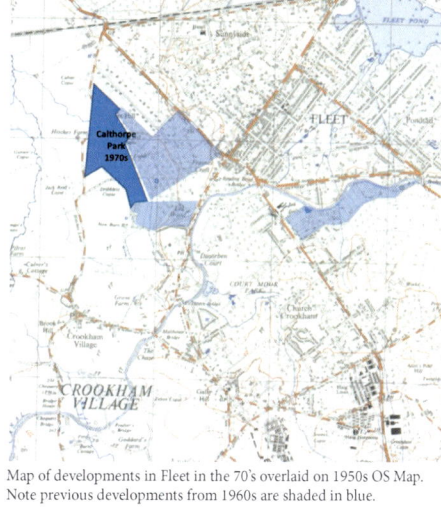

Map of developments in Fleet in the 70's overlaid on 1950s OS Map. Note previous developments from 1960s are shaded in blue.

Keith Monks, prestigious audio supplier from Fleet in the 70's famous for record cleaning equipment.

The Calthorpe Family

Lord Calthorpe and the Elvetham Estate have had a significant impact on the community of Fleet. The area known as Calthorpe Park is a park, a leisure facility and a senior school, which were all developed in the 60's and 70's. The area known as Elvetham Heath was developed in the 2000's. All of these are named after areas either given by the Calthorpe family or sold by the Calthorpe family for significant housing developments.

The stewardship of the family estate is currently overseen by Sir Euan Anstruther-Gough-Calthorpe. Sir Euan is married with four children.

Sir Euan's family have cared for Elvetham since Barbara Reynolds married Reynolds Calthorpe 350 years ago. The Calthorpe and Gough families were later joined when Henry Gough, 2nd Baronet was created 1st Baron Calthorpe in 1796, having inherited Elvetham from Sir Henry Calthorpe, KB in 1788.

100 years later the Hon. Rachel Gough-Calthorpe, who brought great energy and philanthropy to Elvetham, married Sir Fitzroy Hamilton Lloyd-Anstruther. Sir Fitzroy, a Justice of the Peace and First World War veteran, was created 1st Baronet Anstruther-Gough-Calthorpe of Elvetham Hall in 1929. They had a son, Richard, and two daughters, Frances Jean and Barbara. Richard Hamilton A-G-Calthorpe graduated from Cambridge, fought in WWII, rose to Brigadier in the Royal Scots Greys and was decorated with the Croix de Guerre and as a Commander of the Order of the British Empire (CBE). He succeeded to the title of 2nd Baronet of Elvetham Hall in 1957, on the passing of Sir Fitzroy.

Sir Richard's son, Niall Hamilton A-G-Calthorpe, was born on 20 July 1940 but died at the age of 29. Niall's son, Euan Hamilton A-G-Calthorpe, inherited the estate and the 3rd Baronetcy from his grandfather (Sir Richard) in 1985.

Significant gifts to the people of Fleet have included Calthorpe Park sport facilities, donated by Lady Anstruther Gough Calthorpe, and the land for Church on the Heath at Elvetham Heath, donated by Euan Calthorpe.

Road names throughout Fleet that are named in recognition of the Elvetham Estate and the Calthorpe family include: Elvetham Road, Fitzroy Road, Calthorpe Road, Elvetham Heath Way, and Gough Road.

1971

- **January:** Idi Amin seizes power in Uganda.
- **February:** Decimal Day; the United Kingdom introduces a decimalized currency.
- **February:** Rolls Royce goes bust and is bailed out by the British Government.
- **March:** Winnie Mandela goes to prison for a year.
- **August:** Nixon shock removes gold back-up for the US Dollar, triggering export of inflation from rich to poor nations.
- **August:** Internment begins in Northern Ireland.
- **October:** In Orlando, Florida, Walt Disney World opened to worlwide acclaim.
- **November:** Intel releases the world's first microprocessor, the Intel 4004.
- **December:** Third Indo-Pakistani War.
- **December:** At the age of 67, the first person of colour to win a Nobel Peace Prize, Ralph Bunche, passes away.
- **October:** Princess Anne and the Duke of Edinburgh visited Iran to join in the celebrations of the 2500th anniversary of the Persian Empire.

Combined Scout Hut Opened

A bigger scout hut was built to accommodate both 22nd Odiham and 26th Odiham Sea Scouts troops at Calthorpe Park.

Did You Ever Wear?

The 1970's was the decade of flares. Originally flared trousers were worn by American sailors as it was easier to grab a man who had fallen overboard, by grabbing the bottom of his trousers. But it was the music scene, and growing adulation of pop-stars, that caused fashion designers to capitalise on the growing craze for bigger and bigger flares. Mary Quant was influencing a generation of fashion designers and just take a look at what David Essex was wearing!

Calthorpe Park School Officially Opened

The official opening took place on Friday 18th June 1971 by Mr W. van Straubenzee, MBE, MP from the Department of Education and Science. After the National Anthem and a Dedication from the Vicar of Fleet, the Rev A.C.B. Deedes, speeches were given by a variety of people connected to the school including the Chairman of the School Governors, Major B.C. Debenham, MBE, the Chairman of Hampshire County Council, Brig Sir Richard A-G Calthorpe, BT, CBE and Mr Ormerod the school headmaster.

The school formed part of the 1967/68 Major Building Programme, designed by the County Architect in the SCOLA Mark IA form of construction. using standard components with some brick cladding. The total building cost of the project, including fees, furniture and equipment, was approximately £410,000

The original buildings were extended over the years with Phase 2 (English, Tech, Library) being built in 1974, followed by the Maths block, the old and new Drama blocks and of course the Leisure Centre next door.

Mr C. Heasman took over as Headteacher in 1988 before retiring in 2005 when Mrs C. Anwar replaced him. Mr M. Amos and Ms M. Hooper were appointed Joint Headteachers in 2014, retiring in 2021.

Mr K John is now the school's Headteacher and there are currently 1435 students attending.

1972

- **January:** The United Kingdom signs the Treaty of Accession in a ceremony in Brussels which was attended by Prime Minister Edward Heath in preparedness for membership of the European Communities from 1 January 1973.
- **January:** Northern Ireland's Bloody Sunday.
- **May:** Queen's uncle Edward VIII, who abdicated in 1936, died in France.

- **May:** The airplane serving Sabena Flight 571 from Brussels to Lod, Tel Aviv is hijacked by four members of the Black September Organization, a Palestinian terrorist group, resulting in 3 deaths and 3 injuries.
- **September:** The Munich massacre of the Israeli Olympic Team is perpetrated by the Black September terrorist organization and results in 17 total deaths.
- **November:** The arcade game Pong, the first commercially successful video game, is released.

Peter Driver Road Races

The first Peter Driver Road Race was held in memory of Peter Driver 1932-1971. Initially 6 miles in length, the race has gone on to become the Fleet 10k and has been held most years since 1972. Peter was a British track and field athlete and won a gold medal in 1954. In a further honour to Peter a sports hall was built in Church Crookham and named in his memory in 1974. The Peter Driver hall has since been replaced by a care home, but the sports fields associated with the hall is still known as the Peter Driver sports ground.

Crookham Rovers

The original football club, founded in 1972 by Terry Jeal, was called Ferndale Rovers and trained at Queens Avenue. In 1974 they changed their name to Crookham Rovers.

Tavistock Infants Opens

The school, then called North Fleet County Infant School, opened on 17 April 1972, admitting 61 children aged 5-6 years. It cost £90,000 to build. The Head Teacher appointed to the school was Miss Anne C. Walton. The teaching staff consisted of head teacher, deputy head teacher and two assistant teachers. The non-teaching staff consisted of caretaker, cook-in-charge, secretary, two kitchen helpers, three supervisory assistants and a cleaner.

New building of Fleet Methodist church opens on Reading Road South

The present Fleet Methodist Church was opened and dedicated on Saturday 22nd July 1972, marking the culmination of seven years of prayerful planning and fundraising by the congregations of the Reading Road and Fleet Road churches to create a United Methodist Society in Fleet.

Princess Anne at Crookham Horse Trials Tweseldown

Princess Anne, like her mother, is a great lover of

horses. She has competed at the highest levels in three-day eventing, including the 1976 Olympics. As an important location in the eventing calendar she has on several occasions ridden at Tweseldown. The first of these recorded occasions was in 1972.

Fleet joins Hartley Witney to become Hart District

By 1972, the reorganisation of local government was causing a lot of heartaches and although many thought Fleet would join Aldershot and Farnborough, it swung the other way and went in with Hartley Wintney to become Hart District. There was a champagne party in the Victoria Hall at Hartley Wintney at the announcement.

1973

- **January:** The United Kingdom joins and becomes a member state of the European Communities.
- **January:** The Supreme Court of the United States decides Roe v. Wade.
- **March:** Pink Floyd's album The Dark Side of the Moon is released in the UK.
- **May:** The first space station, Skylab, is launched.
- **October:** 1973 oil crisis.
- **October:** Yom Kippur War.
- **November:** Princess Anne marries Captain Mark Phillips at Westminster Abbey, and is the first of Queen's children to marry.

- **December:** Pioneer 10 sends back the first close-up images of Jupiter.

Fleet Assembly Halls Opened

In 1971 work commenced on the Assembly Hall, Library and Car Parks, and when completed comprised one larger hall subsequently named Chernock Hall after the house which for many years housed the public library. A small hall, named 'The Carnival Hall' in recognition of ten thousand pounds donated towards the cost by the Fleet & District Carnival Committee, comprised three committee rooms, kitchens and usual offices, and car parks to accommodate over 200 vehicles. They were officially opened in 1973.

Fleet Urban District Council purchases Fleet Pond from the Ministry of Defence.

The Fleet Division of Girlguiding formed.

The Fleet Division of Girlguiding split away from the Aldershot division and became the Fleet, Crookham and Crondall Division.

Fleet Rememberance Memorial moved

The aftermath of the First World War saw the biggest single wave of public commemoration ever, with tens of thousands of memorials erected across England. One such memorial was raised at Fleet, as a permanent testament to the sacrifice made by the members of the local community, who lost their lives in the First World War. It was built by S Mardles and Sons, and was unveiled in 1920. After the Second World War further inscriptions were added, to commemorate the combatants who lost their lives.

Original Tweseldown Infant School Built

Tweseldown Infants was originally located in Tweseldown Road and was built in 1973.

Fleet Service Station Opens

To many people outside of Fleet, our most famous landmark is "Fleet Services". When it opened in 1973, its simple and spacious layout was praised for being the antidote to the overcrowded and unpleasant services

which had opened so far. It was one of the last services to open with a Grill & Griddle, with blue plastic seats and neatly-laid tables and Scandinavian-style chip-wood ceiling. The café had a décor of green and mauve, with large windows and the illusion of a high-pitched ceiling which created a spacious environment.

The buildings weren't even big enough to connect to the footbridge - the internal connection at each end was provided in the 1980s, and would later blend seamlessly with the rest of the buildings. Following a major fire in 2016, the buildings were replaced and refurbished in 2018

1974

- **WORLD POPULATION REACHES FOUR BILLION.**
- **March: First close-up images of Mercury by Mariner 10.**
- **March: Harold Wilson becomes Prime Minister for the second time.**

- **August: Resignation of Richard Nixon; Vice President Gerald Ford assumes office as President of the United States, the first person not elected as either President or Vice President to take the role.**

- **September: Emperor Haile Selassie I of Ethiopia is overthrown in a military coup.**

Did you admit to liking Abba?

Back in the day it was very uncool to admit that you actually liked Abba's music.

However, they have an enduring legacy as one of the most successful pop groups ever, far beyond other 'cool' bands of the 70s. As the 70's generation have grown older they now feel more comfortable enjoying the Mama Mia franchise and many have recently bought tickets to see avatars of Abba playing in "live" concerts. 1974 was the year it all began for Abba when they won the European Song Contest with the hit "Waterloo".

 Hart District Council

Fleet views from 1970s

Hart District Council was created (under the Local Government Act 1972) as a merger of Fleet Urban District Council and Hartley Wintney Rural District.

Chernocke House (Old Fleet Library)

Demolished

Chernocke House, was a doctor's house and surgery until the late 1920s. From the late 1930s it was split into flats. Its final use was as the public library before being demolished when the present library was completed adjacent to the assembly Halls.

Calthorpe Park Sports Golf and Tennis Opened

On 4 June 1946 the Honourable Dame Rachel Anstruther-Gough-Calthorpe (Lady Calthorpe) signed a deed of gift giving the park to the then Fleet Urban District Council.

The land was given to the people of Fleet with a strict requirement that it would always be used for public park and recreation activities. If it ceased to be used for these purposes the land would revert to Lord Calthorpe's Estate.

For a time, Fleet Urban District Council used Calthorpe Park as a landfill refuse tip. During this period the fish pond, shown on the plan that forms part of the deed of gift, was filled. Tipping ceased in 1964 and some time later the Council covered the tip area with soil and roughly levelled the ground. For a while the open space between the tennis courts and the football field was used as a pitch and putt course.

1975

- January: Altair 8800, the first commercially successful personal computer, is released.
- April: Microsoft founded in Albuquerque, New Mexico by Bill Gates and Paul Allen.

- April: The Fall of Saigon ends the Vietnam War.
- June: The United Kingdom chooses to remain a member state of the European Communities in a non-binding referendum.

- November: Juan Carlos I becomes King of Spain.

Hart Male Voice Choir forms

Hart Male Voice Choir was formed in May 1975 with the aims and objectives to develop choral singing to provide entertainment for performers and audiences. Hart MVC has offered the opportunity for men to share their enjoyment of music by singing together. The choir currently has 65 members who perform songs from a varied repertoire with traditional male voice choir songs as well as songs from the shows, operatic pieces, folk songs and classic hymns. Choir tours in response to invitations have included visits to Germany, France, Spain, Holland, Portugal, South Africa and Ireland.

Major General Dudley Johnson VC dies

Major-General Dudley Graham Johnson, VC, CB, DSO & Bar, MC (13 February 1884 – 21 December 1975) was a British Army officer and recipient of the Victoria Cross, the highest award for gallantry in the face of the enemy that can be awarded to British and Commonwealth forces. He was awarded the Victoria Cross following his heroic action as a lieutenant colonel in November 1918 at the very end of the First World War. He lived out his retirement in Church Crookham and is buried in the cemetry at Christ Church. Johnson Way in Church Crookham is named in his honour.

Kingfisher Music Company

Kingfisher music was an iconic music shop that was located at 20 Kings Road Fleet. Many famous bands bought their gear in the shop including the Sex Pistols, Big Country and Brian May. The site is now occupied by a Co-op mini store.

1976

- **April: James Callaghan becomes Prime Minister.**
- **April: Apple 1 is released.**
- **July: State visit of Queen Elizabeth II to the USA marking the bicentenial of the indepenance of the United States.**

- **August: First outbreak of the Ebola virus in Zaire.**
- **September: Death of Mao Zedong.**
- **September: Release of VHS (Video Home System) in Japan.**
- **September: Heather Munnings is born.**
- **September: Britain becomes the first major Western state to be forced to ask to borrow money from the International Monetary Fund.**
- **October: End of Cultural Revolution in China.**

Gulshan Restaurant Opens in Fleet

The Gulshan claims to be the oldest restaurant in the Fleet area. They are probably correct, having been operating continuosly since their opening in 1976.

Girl Guides lease land from Council

Fleet Girl Guides leased a piece of land from Hart District Council to erect a new divisional Headquarters.

Fleet Pond Society Established

Fleet Pond is the largest freshwater lake in Hampshire. The nature reserve has 141 acres (57ha) of varied habitats including heathland, woodland, reedbed and marsh, and is home for many species of birds, butterflies, dragonflies and wild flowers. The

Pond itself is 52 acres (21ha) so covers some 35% of the total area of the reserve.

The Fleet Pond Society is a voluntary group that exists to protect and manage the Fleet Pond Nature reserve.

Fleet Trefoil Guild Begins Meeting

Trefoil Guild, as a Branch of the Guide Association, offers its members personal and social activities whilst supporting Guiding & Scouting. Trefoil Guild meets nationally and is open to men and women over 18 years of age. The guild currently meets in the Willis Hall in Sandy Lane Church Crookham.

1977

- **January:** Jimmy Carter is inaugurated as President of the United States.
- **May:** Star Wars is released and quickly becomes the highest-grossing film of all-time.
- **June:** The Queen celebrates her silver jubilee.

- **August:** Death of Elvis Presley.
- **August:** Voyager 2 launched by NASA.
- **September:** Voyager 1 launched by NASA.
- **September:** Release date of the Atari 2600 video game console in North America.
- **October:** The last wild case of smallpox is eradicated by the WHO.
- **November:** The Queen becaomes a grandmother after her daughter Princess Anne gives birth to a son, Peter Phillips.

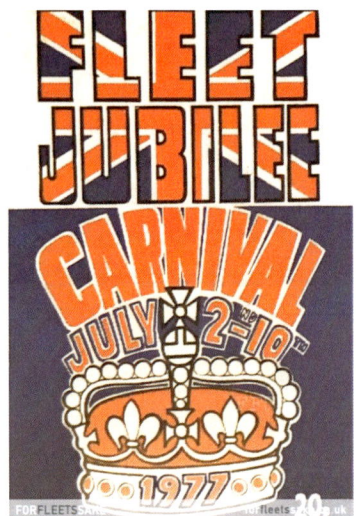

Jubilee Street Parties

Street parties were held throughout Fleet. Church services, parades and town wide celebrations were held at the Views Meadows.

All Children in our schools were given a Silver Jubilee Crown (25p)

Basingstoke Canal Refurbisment Commenced

The Basingstoke Canal, originally built in 1794, had fallen into a state of disrepair and had stopped being used commercially in 1910. The canal was purchased by Hampshire and Surrey councils, from private owners with the threat of a compulsory purchase order in 1976. Restoration of the canal began in 1977 and continued until its full 32 miles length was complete and re-opened in 1991.

Redfields Garden Centre Opens

Crookham was one of the few locations of a commercially successful tobacco plantation in Britain, which produced among other brands "Blue Prior" cigarettes and pipe tobacco. Production finished in 1938 and the plantation site is now occupied by Redfields Garden Centre.

The Brandon family, who owned the estate, mainly grew tobacco and hops. The hot-curing sheds, where they processed the tobacco, were situated where the Redfields Industrial Estate stands now. The estate was not split up until after the Second World War when Mr Brandon died.

Fleet guides acquire an ex-M3 contractors building

A temporary building used by a contractor working on the M3 motorway was acquired by Fleet Guides and re-purposed as a new HQ. The building was moved to Basingbourne Park, from where the Girl Guides still operate.

1978

- **March:** The oil tanker, Amoco Cadiz, runs aground on the coast of Brittany.
- **April:** TV Series Dallas premiers on US TV.

- **June:** Discovery of Pluto's moon Charon.
- **July:** Louise Brown becomes the first human in history to be born via in vitro fertilisation.
- **September:** Pope John Paul I dies after only 33 days of papacy.
- **September:** Invention of artificial insulin.
- **October:** Independence of Tuvalu from Britain.
- **November:** Jim Jones's new religious movement, the People's Temple, ends in the organized mass killing and suicide of 920 people in Jonestown.

Queen Elizabeth inspects Gurkhas

Gurkhas, as always, were immaculately presented

Her Magesty arrived at the Barracks in an open top Landrover

Queen Visits the Gurkhas at Church Crookham

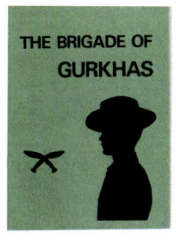

The 6th Queen Elizabeth's Own Gurkha Rifles was a rifle regiment of the British Indian Army comprising Gurkha soldiers of Nepalese origin, before being transferred to the British Army following India's independence. Originally raised in 1817, the name 6th Queen Elizabeth's Own Gurkha Rifles ceased to exist as part of the British Army in 1994. The Queen visited the batallion bearing her name in Church Crookham in 1978.

Do you Remember?

Launched in 1978, Top Trumps was a card game popular with adults and children in the United Kingdom in the 1970s and 1980s, especially among boys, for whom it was a popular playground pastime. The topics tended to reflect this, and included military hardware, modes of transport and racing cars. Top Trumps is enjoying somewhat of a ressurgence and a new generation of children are learning various performance categories. There is even a 2022 Queen Elizabeth II top trump.

1979

- January: The Vietnamese invasion of Kampuchea ends Cambodia's Khmer Rouge regime.
- February: The Iranian Revolution ends. Shah Reza Pahlavi is overthrown and forced into exile.
- March: The Three Mile Island nuclear accident, a partial meltdown of reactor.
- May: Margaret Thatcher becomes

the first female Prime Minister.

- June: Death of John Wayne.
- August: The Queen's second cousin and close friend, Louis Mountbatten, 1st Earl Mountbatten of Burma, is killed by an IRA bomb while on a

fishing boat off the coast of Sligo, Ireland.

- December: The Rhodesian Bush War ends.
- December: The Soviet-Afghan War begins.

Carnival Bridge opens across Fleet Pond

The Carnival Bridge, completing the circuit around Fleet Pond, was opened in July 1979. The bridge cost £500 to build, with funds provided by the Fleet Carnival Committee. In 2011, the 32 year old bridge was re-positioned and revamped. It was officially re-opened by the family of Charles Woodman to which the original bridge was dedicated. The old plaque has been presented to the Fleet and Crookham history group. A new bridge called The Flash has been built alongside Fleet car park and the Brooklyn Bridge has been widened.

Do you remember?

Corona delivery trucks were often seen around the local area, and many children would keep an eye out for a discarded bottle, because there was a 10p deposit for all bottles returned.

Victoria Road looking towards upper street 1979

Do you still know the moves?

Village people scored a massive hit with disco favourite YMCA. The song, that was accompanied with a set of dance moves spelling out YMCA with your arms, was, and still is a massive hit in clubs and dance venues worldwide. The royalties from YMCA are still making several million dollars every year for the songwriter Victor Wills, who sang in the lineup as the motorcycle cop. But do you still remember the dance moves?

1980

- January : Launch of the Rubik's Cube.
- April: Independence of Rhodesia, which becomes Zimbabwe.

- May: WHO announces the eradication of smallpox.

- May: Eruption of Mount St. Helens in Skamania County, Washington, causes approximately 57 deaths and $1 billion of property damage.
- May: The Empire Strikes Back is released.
- August: Solidarity union forms at Poland's Gdańsk Shipyard under Lech Wałęsa, and begins agitation for greater personal freedoms.
- September: Beginning of the Iran-Iraq War.
- November: Ronald Reagan is elected as the 40th President of the United States, the oldest person to be elected.
- November: Voyager 1 takes the first close-up pictures of Saturn.
- December: Murder of John Lennon.

"Map of developments in Fleet in the 1980's overlaid on 1950s OS Map. Note previous developments from 1950s to 1970s are shaded in blue"

Did you own one?

The Sinclair ZX80 was a home computer launched on 29 January 1980 by Science of Cambridge Ltd. (later to be better known as Sinclair Research). It was notable for being one of the first computers available in the United Kingdom for less than a hundred pounds. It was available in kit form for £79.95, where purchasers had to assemble and solder it together, and as a ready-built version at £99.95. The ZX80 was imediately popular, and for some time there was a waiting list of several months for either version of the machine. For many children in 1980s Fleet ZX80 launched a career in computing.

Heatherside Infants Opened

Adjacent to the site of Heatherside juniors a new infant school was built in 1980.

Fleet Town in 1980s

1981

- **March: President Reagan and three others are injured after an assassination attempt.**

- **April: First orbital flight of the Space Shuttle.**
- **May: Queen's eldest granddaughter Zara Phillips (now Tindall) is born to Princess Anne.**

- **June: The Humber Bridge opens, the longest single-span bridge in the world.**
- **June: The AIDS epidemic officially begins in the United States, having originated in Africa.**
- **July: Prince Charles weds Lady Diana Spencer during a ceremony at Westminster Abbey.**

- **August: IBM Personal Computer released.**

Royal wedding train passes through Fleet

Crowds lined the station and every bridge to cheer the train carrying Prince Charles and Lady Diana to start their honeymoon. The same scenes were pictured along the entire length of the railway line between Waterloo and their joining the Royal Yacht Britannia for 14 days of cruising around the mediteranean and Greek Islands.

Although it was only a fleeting glance of the train passing through Fleet, everyone watching felt closer to the beloved Royal couple.

Here it is pictured as it passes through Fleet Station in July 1981.

Church Army Anchorage Home Demolished

The Courtmoor Home for Motherless Boys was opened in 1918 by the Church Army. It occupied a house at the east side of Castle Street. In 1920 the premises could accommodate up to 21 boys, aged 7-11 at the date of admission. It subsequently became a holiday home for poor city children and their mothers. In 1931, it was turned into a home for elderly men which continued in use till 1974. The building was demolished in 1981.

Do you Remember?

Do you remember listening to the Top 40, recording your favourite songs and making sure to press the pause button before the speaking started. Did you ever share your tape with someone special?

1982

- **April:** Israel withdraws from Sinai Peninsula.
- **April:** The Falklands War breaks out and her son, Prince Andrew, is among those serving in the forces. An intruder makes his way into the queen's bedroom in Buckingham Palace but leaves without incident.

- **June:** Prince William was born at St Mary's Hospital, London on 21st June as the first child of Charles, Prince of Wales, making him second in line to the throne.

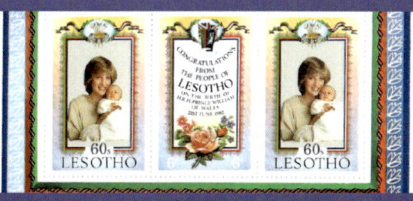

- **September:** Princess Grace of Monaco dies following a car accident.
- **October:** Sony releases the world's first commercially sold CD Player, the Sony CDP-101.
- **November:** Death of Leonid Brezhnev; Yuri Andropov becomes General Secretary of the Communist Party of the Soviet Union.
- **November :** Channel 4 launches across most of England, Scotland and Northern Ireland.
- **December:** The first execution by lethal injection takes place in Texas.

First Lions Firework Display

The first community firework display, originally held at The Views in Fleet and now held regularly at Calthorpe Park, was organised, and continues to be organised, by Fleet Lions, raising funds for good works around the town.

Velmead School Damaged by Fire

The original Velmead school was severely damaged following an arson attack in 1982.

First Fleet Half Marathon

The first Fleet Half Marathon took place on Sunday 4th April 1982, a year after the first London Marathon. That year there were 1995 finishers, an amazing number for a new event. It was won by D Stevens from Hastings AC with a time of 65:32 and the first woman to finish was local runner Paula Fudge in a time of 72.31, coming in 30th place overall.

In the early days the event was run out of Rushmoor military arena in Aldershot. The Red Devils jumped in and the Band of the Gurkhas played.

Going forward, the event was given permission by Chris Brasher, organiser of the London Marathon and a friend of prime Fleet Half Marathon organiser Colin Gostelow, to be known as "the pre-London" half marathon. The event grew and remained at its base on the edge of Aldershot until 1993, when it relocated to Calthorpe Park. Starting and finishing now in the town, it truly was the Fleet Pre-London Half Marathon. The foundations had been laid for a very successful race to become a premier event in the town's calendar and on the local running scene. Thousands of people have taken part in the years since.

Oasis Flower Shop opened in Fleet

The Oasis Flower shop opened in Fleet in 1982, and continues to bring colour and fragrance to Fleet Road today.

Falklands Gurkha Parade

Returning to the UK on the SS Uganda, the Gurkhas marched through Fleet on 9th August 1992, ninety days after they had left Southampton on the QE2. The Gurkhas deployed in 1982 with 5th Infantry Brigade as part of the task force which successfully recaptured the Falkland Islands following the Argentine invasion. The Division's primary action was at Mount William, thereby earning its final Battle Honour.

The Battalion was once again in the United Kingdom from 1991 for what would be its final years, until it was amalgamated in 1994 with both battalions of 2nd King Edward VII's Own Gurkha Rifles (The Sirmoor Rifles), 6th Queen Elizabeth's Own Gurkha Rifles, and 10th Princess Mary's Own Gurkha Rifles to form the Royal Gurkha Rifles.

At a final parade at Church Crookham on 26 May 1994, attended by HRH The Duke of Edinburgh and many old comrades from Britain and Nepal, the Regiment "marched into history."

1983

- **January:** Independence of Brunei.
- **January:** Seatbelt use for drivers and front seat passengers becomes mandatory in the United Kingdom.
- **March:** China's population reaches 1 Billion.
- **March:** President Reagan and Queen Elizabeth II toasted one another at a dinner in the Queens honour.

- **August:** Motorola Introduced the first "mobile" phones. The price was $3,995.
- **October:** Richard Noble sets a new land speed record of 633.468 mph, driving Thrust 2 at the Black Rock Desert, Nevada.

- **November:** Brinks Mat warehouse robbery at Heathrow Airport - thieves made off with three tons of gold bars valued at $37.5 million.

Episode of the Professionals filmed at Queen Elizabeth Barracks

The Professionals, featuring detectives "Bodie" and "Doyle", filmed an episode at the Queen Elizabeth Barracks in 1983.

Guides HQ Officially Opened in Basignbourne Road

Crookham Village

Since 1983 Crookham Village has been twinned with Lévignen in France. Lévignen is about 40 miles North East of Paris, near Crépy-en-Valois, Senlis and the forest of Compiegne.

Fleet Bible Bookshop Opened

In 1983 a group of Churches in Fleet came together to establish "Fleet Bible Bookshop". This was initially in reaction to the possibility of the opening of a Sex Shop on Fleet Road, and wanting to offer local Christians access to books and other "uplifting" material. This venture was established as a charity and in 1994 opened as a much larger Christian Centre that is now called LivingStones Christian Centre. The centre has a mission to build community and incorporates a cafe and community rooms as well as continuing to supply Christian resources. As of 2022, the centre is run by volunteers and all of the revenue it generates are donated to local charities.

1984

- **March:** The UK miners' strike takes place to prevent Margaret Thatcher's government from closing down the British coal mining industry.
- **April:** The human immunodeficiency virus (HIV) is recognized as the cause of AIDS, and research on zidovudine and other treatments gets underway.

- **September:** Princess Diana and Prince Charles' second son, Prince Harry, was born on the 15th September 1984 in the Lindo Wing of St Mary's Hospital in Paddington, London.
- **October:** Assassination of Indira Gandhi, Indian Prime Minister.
- **December:** Sino-British Joint Declaration agrees to hand Hong Kong back to China by 1997.

Kentucky Fried Chicken Moves from Reading Road South

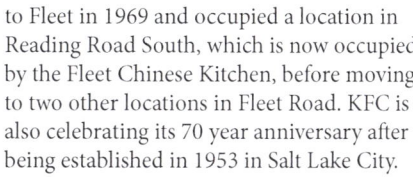

The first KFC restuarant in the UK opened in 1965. Kentucky Fried Chicken first came to Fleet in 1969 and occupied a location in Reading Road South, which is now occupied by the Fleet Chinese Kitchen, before moving to two other locations in Fleet Road. KFC is also celebrating its 70 year anniversary after being established in 1953 in Salt Lake City.

First passage through Fleet of the canal boat "John Pinkerton"

The Canal Society's trip boat "John Pinkerton" began operating in Odiham in 1978 and passed through Fleet for the first time in March 1984.

Dredging takes place in the Fleet stretch of the Basingstoke Canal

Fleet Carnival grows from strength to strength as all the community get involved.

1985

- January: First use of DNA fingerprinting.
- March: Mikhail Gorbachev becomes General Secretary of the Communist Party of the Soviet Union.
- July: Live Aid Concert.
- September: 73 years after the infamous disaster, the wreck of the Titanic is found off the coast of Newfoundland by a joint French-American expedition led by Jean-Louis Michel of IFREMER and Robert Ballard of the Woods Hole Oceanographic Institution.
- October: Release date of the Macintosh 128K, the first successful mass-market personal computer to feature a graphical user interface, built-in screen, and mouse.
- November: Windows 1.0, the first Microsoft Windows operating system, released.
- November: Charles and Diana party at the White House, Washington with the Reagans. Diana was the "belle of the ball".

Feargal Sharkey OBE - Famous Resident

Feargal Sharkey, lead vocalist of the Undertones, was a resident in Queens Road, Fleet during 1985.

The Fleet War Memorial moved from behind the library to Gurkha Square.

The Fleet War Memorial moved to its current location in Gurkha Square, which is so named to commemorate the long association of the town with the Gurkha Regiment.

Fleet and Crookham Local History Group Established

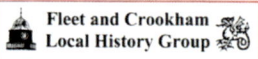

The Fleet and Crookham Local History Group began meeting in October 1985, and as well as presenting a variety of items of local history, they have diligently built an archive of local historical papers, artefacts and photographs, some of which can be seen in the Fleet Library Heritage Zone.

The Queens Platinum Jubilee Committee acknowledge the great help FCLHG have provided in preparing these posters.

Princess Anne at the Races

Princess Anne was in Tweseldown again in 1985 for the Crookham Races. Tweseldown was originally a National Hunt steeplechasing venue and the home for equestrian dressage and eventing competitions. Until 2012 the venue hosted point to point racing, but due to lack of funds racing had to halt, although horse trials continue.

1986

- January: First close-up images of the planet Uranus.
- January: Challenger breaks apart 73 seconds into its flight, killing all seven crew members aboard.
- February: End of dictatorship of Ferdinand Marcos in the Philippines.
- March: Return of Halley's Comet.
- April: The first child born to a non-related surrogate mother is born.
- April: The United Kingdom and the Kingdom of the Netherlands sign a peace treaty, thus ending the Three Hundred and Thirty Five Years' War, one of the longest wars in human history.
- April: The Chernobyl disaster in Ukraine kills about 100 people.
- April: Wallis Simpson, Duchess of Windsor and wife of ex-King Edward VIII, dies.
- July: Prince Andrew marries Sarah Ferguson and becomes Duke of York.

Stars Turn out for Half Marathon

The Fleet and Crookham half marathon for 1986 attracted a plethora of stars from stage and screen. Among the big names running in 1986 were Toyah Wilcox, Kenny Lynch and Billy J Kramer. They were all running as part of the TV Times Allinsons Leukaemia Reasearch Team. All of the stars managed to finish the 13.1 mile course.

Accessible Boating Introduced on Basingstoke Canal

In recognising that the Basingstoke Canal should be open to all, a charity was formed in 1986 (originally called Boats for the Handicapped), with the goal of raising funds to provide a day boat with wheelchair access that would be able to operate on the canal. In July 1986, following a competition held to select a name, the first Accessible Boating Association (ABA) canal boat was launched by Lady de Knayth and named "The Mildred Stocks". Mildred had been a local councillor who had actively supported the ambitions of the charity.

2nd Fleet Boys Brigade begins meeting at Fleet Methodist Church

Boys' Brigade is an international organisation over 125 years old, and 2nd Fleet Company has been running at FMC since 1986. They meet every Wednesday evening in term time and they work together to find fun ways to learn and encourage the development of a personal Christian faith.

Fleet Infants School Moves to Velmead Road

The original Fleet School was built in 1860 and was run from a cottage in Church Road. The school expanded very quickly and was taken over by the Church in 1863. By 1885 it had grown to 120 pupils and needed to expand again so 18 plots of land on the corner of Albert Street and Church Road were purchased and a set of new school buildings constructed. The infant section of the school was constucted in 1910, utilising the Church Road plots of land. In 1947, following the constuction of Heatherside school the seniors left the Fleet School and enrolled at Heatherside Secondary Modern. Following the constuction of Courtmoor the juniors also left the site, leaving Fleet School to become Albert Street Infants. Finally the remaining infant school was moved to Velmead in 1987 to what was initially called Velmead Infants and then renamed Fleet Infants.

The new infant school was designed by Hopkins and Partners in 1984-1985, and built in 1985-1986 for Hampshire County Council. It has become a listed building for reasons of architectural interest, as "an inventive and engaging solution to the design of an infant school by a leading architectural practice", and constructional interest, as "a predominantly glazed, light-weight steel frame".

The old school site was demolished and made way for what is now called "Old School Close".

1987

WORLD POPULATION REACHES FIVE BILLION.

- **January:** Terry Waite, the special envoy of the Archbishop of Canterbury, was kidnapped in Beirut.
- **March:** The first Starbucks outside of the US is opened in Vancouver, Canada.
- **March:** Zeebrugge disaster: Roll-on/roll-off cross-channel ferry MS Herald of Free Enterprise capsizes off Zeebrugge harbor in Belgium; 193 people die.
- **May:** Crowd of 800,000+ packed onto the Golden Gate Bridge and its approaches for its 50th Anniversary celebration.
- **October:** Stock market crash of 1987.

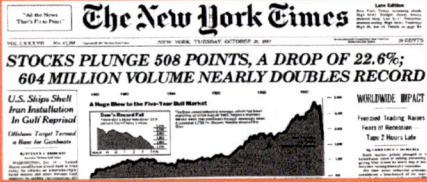

- **November:** The InterCity 125 breaks the world speed record for a diesel-powered train, reaching 238 km/h (147.88 mph)
- **December:** Windows 2.0 released.

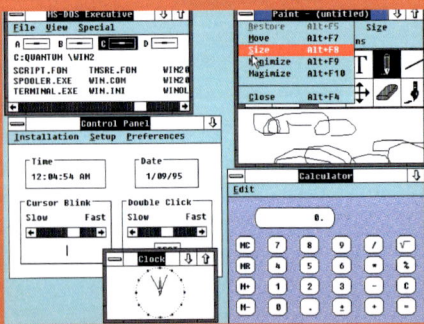

All Saints Church and Christ Church become Grade II listed buildings

The main Fleet Parish Church was built in 1862 by William Burgess with additions in 1934 and a "modern" extension (including a Lady Chapel in 1958). Christ Church in Crookham had pre-dated All Saints Church, being built in 1841, and the Lefroy family played a central role in building both Churches, with Charles Lefroy and his wife Janet being memorialised through a monument in the North West of All Saints Church. Lefroy's nephew Anthony Cottrell Lefroy was the first curate at Christ Church. Christ Church became a listed building 1993 whilst for All Saints it was 1987.

Plans Finalised and Approved for the Hart Centre

In December 1987 developers Bredero Properties presented and were given approval for the "Hart Shopping Centre". The original plans included a four level complex with a supermarket, restaurant, pub, 37 shops and 523 parking spaces. In the original plans, Frisby's shoe shop would be demolished to make way for one entrance with Unwins off-license and the next-door opticians and bakers forming the other. When the plans were originally presented the chairman of the Fleet Chamber of Commerce Mr. Bryan Sheppard was reported as saying, "something like this can only be a good thing for the shoppers of Fleet".

Fleet hit by Huge Storm Winds

On 15th October 1987 one of the biggest storms to hit Britain in 50 years swept across the nation. The powerful storm which hit parts of the UK overnight 15/16 October 1987, became infamous in the country. Winds gusted up to 100mph, causing major destruction, particularly across Southern England. Eighteen people were killed and at least 15 million trees were blown down. Fleet suffered significant damage from falling trees and power was lost for some people for several days. Many substantial oak trees were felled, including in Fleet. In trying to make light of the damage, it was suggested that Seven Oaks in Kent should be renamed Three Oaks!

Fleet Carnival Celebrating 50 years of Television

The theme of the 1987 Carnival was "50 years of Television". The procession was one of the longest seen at the carnival with many creative ideas celebrating television characters from the past 50 years. The cover of the carnival programme featured "Bill and Ben" and of course "Weed" from the "Flowepot Men".

1988

- **January:** Beginning of the perestroika ("restructuring"), a political movement for reformation within the Communist Party of the Soviet Union associated with Gorbachev and his glasnost ("openness") policy reform.

- **January:** Construction of the Channel Tunnel begins.
- **March:** The Liberal Democrats are founded.
- **August:** End of the Iran-Iraq War.
- **October:** Matilda by Roald Dahl is published.
- **October:** Release date of the Mega Drive video game console in Japan.
- **November:** George H. W. Bush is elected President of the United States.

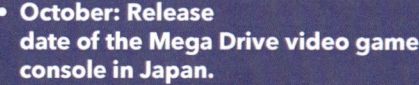

- **December:** Pan Am Flight 103 crashes over Lockerbie, Scotland, killing 270 people and leaving no survivors.

Technograph and Telegraph move to Bracknell

The old building that was occupied by Technograph and Telegraph was demolised in 1988 to make way for the nightclub and Waitrose components of the Hart shopping centre. Technograph and Telegraph were a significant employer in Fleet, making printed circuit boards. In 1977 they moved to Bracknell.

RAE renamed Royal Aircraft Establishment

RAE Farnborough was one of the areas biggest employers. Established in Farnbborough in 1904 initially as a balloon factory, it became the national focus for powered aircraft and in 1908 was the site of the first powered flight by Samuel Cody. It was renamed the Royal Aircraft Factory, but following the end of the First World War was renamed the Royal Aircraft Establishment (RAE) to avoid any confusion with the now established RAF. In 1988 the name was formally changed from RAE to the Royal Aircraft Establishment. In 1991 it was merged into the Defence Research Agency (DRA) and then in 1995 became the Defence Evaluation and Research Agency (DERA). In 2001 it was part-privatised and became part of defence company QinetiQ.

Fleet Cycling Tourist Club

Fleet Cycling Tourist Club (CTC) began in the late eighties as the Fleet branch of the national cycling club, drawing together cycling enthusiats across the town. Renamed now as Fleet Cycling, the club has over 200 members and welcomes riders of all abilities. Organised rides happen throughout the week starting from the Leisure centre, although in the 80's the start point was the Oatsheaf.

1989

- **January:** Emperor Shōwa (Hirohito) dies; his son, Akihito (the Emperor Heisei) becomes Emperor of Japan.
- **February:** End of the Soviet war in Afghanistan.
- **March:** The oil tanker Exxon Valdez spills 10.8 million US gallons of crude oil after striking a reef, causing severe damage to the environment.
- **April:** Tiananmen Square Massacre, in which troops armed with assault rifles and accompanied by tanks fired at student-led demonstrations held in Tiananmen Square, Beijing, results in an undisclosed number of deaths (estimated in hundreds to thousands).
- **April:** Release date of the Game Boy handheld console in Japan.
- **October:** Queen Elizabeth II and Duke of Edinburgh tour Singapore.
- **November:** Fall of the Berlin Wall; the Revolutions of 1989 and the collapse of the Soviet Bloc begin in Europe, which leads to the end of the Cold War.
- **December:** Trial and execution of Nicolae and Elena Ceaușescu in Romania.

Fugelmere Probus Club Established

10th April 1989, Fugelmere Probus Club of Fleet held it first monthly luncheon. Fugelmere was the second Probus Club established in Fleet for retired businessmen and professionals. It has survived and prospered; continuing to welcome new members from across our community.

There was a significant waiting list of prospective members for Fleet Probus which had been originally sponsored by the Rotary Club of Fleet. Rotary established Probus Clubs to cater for retired businessmen and professionals. It was decided to establish a second Probus Club in Fleet and the name eventually chosen was Fugelmere Probus, the name Fugelmere derived from a name long associated with Fleet Pond.

Fleet Probus collapsed in recent years, a number of members joined Fugelmere whilst others established the new club Phoenix Probus, which continues to meet at the North Hants Golf Club.

Pearsons Corner Auction House Closes

Up until 1989, Fleet used to have its own auction house selling everything from fine arts to bric-a-brac. The auction room was demolished but one building still stands at the junction between Kings Road and Fleet Road at a corner that is still known as Pearson's corner. The closure was triggered by the purchase of Pearson's by the Prudential.

Death of Daphne du Maurier

In the late 1930s Daphne du Maurier lived in Church Crookham in a house called Greyfriars that used to stand in Gables Road. In honour of her association with the area, various du Maurier-related names were chosen for the Zebon Copse development, when it was built in the 1990s. These roads included Danvers Drive, Daphne Drive, Rebecca Close, Du Maurier Close and Frenchmans Creek. In addition, Browning road and Browning close were named after her husband Lieutenant-General Fredrick Browning.

1990

- **February: Nelson Mandela is released from Victor Verster Prison outside Cape Town, South Africa after 27 years as a political prisoner.**

- **April : Launch of the Hubble Space Telescope.**
- **May: Queen Elizabeth II attends Royal Windsor Horse Show.**

- **May: Windows 3.0 released.**
- **August: Gulf War begins.**
- **October: German reunification.**
- **November : John Major becomes Prime Minister.**
- **December: Tim Berners-Lee publishes the first web site, which described the World Wide Web project.**
- **December: The Intergovernmental Panel on Climate Change releases its first assessment report, linking increases in carbon dioxide in the Earth's atmosphere, and a resultant rise in global temperature, to human activities.**

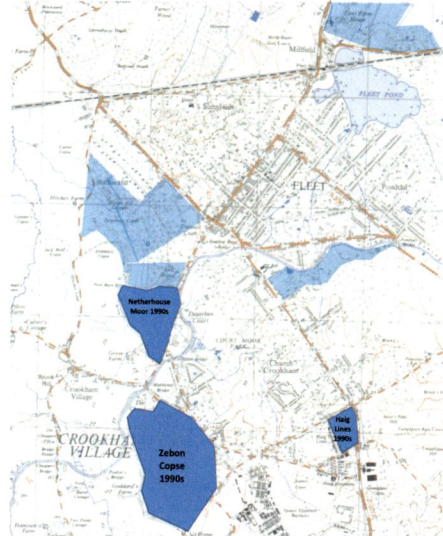

Map of developments in Fleet in the 1990's overlaid on 1950s OS Map. Note previous developments from 1950s to 1980s are shaded in blue

Hart Road Runners Formed

Hart Road Runners are a friendly, inclusive running club that attracts runners from Fleet, Church Crookham and surrounding area. Hart Road Runners was formed by a small group of running enthusiasts who wanted to train together for the first Fleet Half Marathon in 1982. In those first few years the club was know as "Fleet Run for Fun Club". Over the next few years the club went from strength to strength and around 1990 changed their name to "Hart Road Runners". The club's objective has always been to encourage and promote amateur road and cross country in an inclusive and supportive environment. The club caters for all standards, from those who can just run a 5km to those who might be classed as semi-elite.

County Commercial Tractors Closing

Founded in 1929, the company Commercial Tractors faced financial difficulty in 1983 and was bought by Benson Group, who transferred most production to Knighton. The last County produced was a County 1184 tractor but instead of the old County Blue colour it was finished in the Knighton red. A plaque is now located on the building where factory used to be. Much of the ground occupied by the old buildings are now the Hart Centre.

1991

- **February:** The Gulf War ends in US withdrawal and a failed uprising.

- **April:** Polish State visit to the UK. The Queen meets with Lech Walesa.
- **May:** Helen Sharman becomes the first British person and the first European woman in space.
- **June:** The Ten-Day War in Slovenia begins the Yugoslav Wars.
- **July:** Boris Yeltsin becomes the first President of Russia.
- **October:** Linus Torvalds launches the first version of the Linux kernel.
- **November:** Death of Freddie Mercury, British singer, songwriter, and record producer.
- **December:** Dissolution of the Soviet Union and independence of 15 former Soviet republics.

SD-SCICON becomes EDS

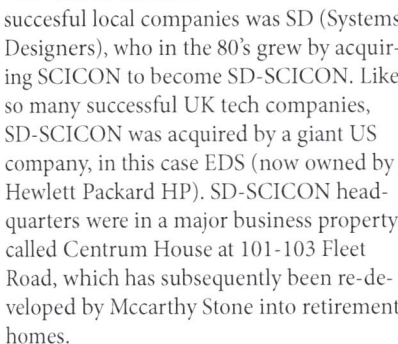

Fleet was a major tech hub in the 80's and 90's. One of our most succesful local companies was SD (Systems Designers), who in the 80's grew by acquiring SCICON to become SD-SCICON. Like so many successful UK tech companies, SD-SCICON was acquired by a giant US company, in this case EDS (now owned by Hewlett Packard HP). SD-SCICON headquarters were in a major business property called Centrum House at 101-103 Fleet Road, which has subsequently been re-developed by Mccarthy Stone into retirement homes.

Fleet Rugby Football Club Formed

Now known as Aldershot & Fleet, the club has come a long way in their short history. The club started in 1991 as a pub side when twelve players would meet on a Saturday morning and grab anyone else around to make up a squad. Many of these early players are still active members of the Club.

Basingstoke Canal Officially Reopened by HRH Duke of Kent

The Basingstoke Canal was officially reopened by HRH The Duke of Kent, accompanied by Society chairman Robin Higgs, at a ceremony at Frimley Lodge Park on 10th May 1991. The following day two convoys of boats set out, one going westwards to the end of the navigation at North Warnborough, and the other, headed by the John Pinkerton, setting off eastwards before dawn, finally reaching the junction with the River Wey at West Byfleet in the late afternoon after a series of civic welcomes.

Hart Leisure Centre Expansion Opens

Hart Leisure Centre was originally built in 1968 in a location next to Calthorpe Park School. The centre went through significant expansion in 1991 to provide a 25m 6 lane swimming pool, 13m learner pool, 5 court sports hall, 3 court sports hall, fitness suite and 6 squash courts. As the population of Fleet has continued to grow, it eventually outgrew the capacity of this leisure centre and so a new centre was commisioned and built across the road on the edge of the Edenbrook Country Park. Calthorpe Park school continues to make use of the sports halls that were associated with the original centre.

Hart Shopping Centre opened by Duchess of York

Two developments in Fleet involved a double opening on 10 May 1991; the Hart Shopping Centre, which was opened officially by the Duchess Of York, and on the same day, she also attended the opening of the Hart Leisure Centre on Hitches Lane.

1992

- February: The Maastricht Treaty creates the European Union. It takes effect on November 1st 1993.
- April: End of dictatorship in Albania.
- April: The Bosnian War begins.
- April: Los Angeles riots over the acquittal of those involved in the beating of Rodney King.
- April: John Major wins election to remain Prime Minister.
- September: Black Wednesday - the Pound and Italian Lira are forced out of European Exchange Rate Mechanism.
- December: The Queen describes it "annus horribilis". Her daughter, Princess Anne, and Capt Phillips divorce. Meanwhile, the Waleses and the Yorks also separate. Windsor Castle, the Queen's primary residence, suffers an extensive fire.

M3 Junction 4A Opens

The M3, originally conceived as the London to Basingstoke Motorway, was built to relieve traffic on the A30 and A33. The early parts opened in two phases in 1971 and 1974 covering the route between J1 to J8. In 1992, Farnborough and Fleet were given their own dedicated 4A junction. Further development of this junction resulted in a private exit off the northern roundabout used to provided access to the UK headquarters of Sun Microsystems at Guillemont Park in 2000; however, this has now been converted into a housing estate.

Dakotas Opens and Aircraft in Pond

Dakotas American Bistro and Bar opened on the 29th April 1992. The building was purpose built for the new American Bistro on open land near to the Country Club (no longer in existence) near Fleet Pond. The restaurant was known for its dark wood interior with nostalgic brass features but also for the rather quirky decor. Sections of a real Dakota plane were used to decorate the interior of the restaurant - the main undercarriage leg, tailwheel and refurbished R1830-92 engine were put on display in the bar.

The tail end of the plane was placed in the lake next to the building as an advertising stunt, highlighting the name of the new restaurant. It became headline news when shocked passersby reported that a plane had crashed in the lake. The plane was eventually removed.

Death of Mabel Frances Wickham

Mabel Frances Wickham was an artist and teacher born in Fleet in 1901. She was recorded as saying, "to me painting is learning to see." Her parents encouraged her talent and from 1919–23 she studied in the art department of Clapham High School, including a year's teacher training, then taught art at Lord Digby's School, Sherborne. By the early 1930s she had opted to teach part-time to develop her own painting, for 14 years attending summer landscape painting courses run by St Clair Marston. She was elected to the Society of Women Artists in 1936, showed regularly at the Royal Academy and with local groups such as Sherborne Art Club.

On retiring in 1953 Wickham moved to Weymouth, Dorset. She ran her own summer courses and lectured for the Workers' Educational Association, Bristol Extra-Mural Department and Portland Bill Observatory; she travelled widely, including the Near East; and attended John Nash's botanical illustration course at Flatford Mill Field Study Centre.

Velmead Community Centre Opens

The Velmead Community Centre, now called the Zebon Community Centre, was opened in 1992. It has been extended twice, initially in 1996 by the addition of a second hall to support the building of the second phase of the Zebon Copse estate. The Centre was taken over by the Parish Council in 2009 and was further extended to add a stage and storage facilities.

1993

- **January: Velvet Divorce between Czech Republic and Slovakia.**
- **January: Bill Clinton is inaugurated as President of the United States.**

- **February: World Trade Center bombing.**
- **April: The Waco siege, the law enforcement siege of the compound that belonged to the Seventh-day Adventist religious sect Branch Davidians near Waco, Texas, carried out by the U.S. federal government, Texas state law enforcement, and the U.S. military, which results in a gunfight, a fire at the compound and 86 deaths.**

- **May: Queen entertains President Mary Robinson of Republic of Ireland.**
- **June: Queen Elizabeth II celebrates 40th Anniversary of her Coronation.**
- **July: Release date of Windows NT 3.1.**

Canal dredging completed

Completion of dredging of the Basingstoke Canal in Hampshire by the steam dredger "Perseverance" and volunteer members of the Surrey & Hampshire Canal Society.

Chadney Bulgin Established in Fleet

Chadney Bulgin, based in Fleet, Hampshire, was founded in 1993 by Tom Chadney (who retired in 2005) and Bruce Bulgin. The firm has acquired five other companies since it began. The firm has been in Fleet since its establishment and has been located at 89 Fleet Road. The business was acquired in October 2021 by Fairstone and is now trading under that name at the same location in Fleet Road.

Benson House Dental Practice Opens

Benson House opened as a private dental practice in 1993. The practise, is now a BUPA practice called Oasis Dental Care. Benson House has a long Fleet history. Before it became known as "Benson House", 37 Kings Road was called "Rosario" and was owned between 1880 and 1974 by the Frewer family. The original plot of land was purchased for £170 and building costs for Rosario were £1100. It was a grand house indeed as can be evidenced by the quality of the stain glass windows that remain at the dental practice.

Hart Shopping Centre Sold to Frogmore Estates

Frogmore Estates, the property investor and developer, acquired the freehold on the Hart shopping centre in Fleet, Hampshire, for £13.3m from Norwich Union. The centre was later sold in 1996 to Bourne End Properties for £18.65m.

1994

- May: End of apartheid in South Africa and election of Nelson Mandela.
- May: The Channel Tunnel opens, the first physical connection between the United Kingdom and France.

- July: Amazon founded in Bellevue, Washington by Jeff Bezos.
- July: Death and state funeral of Kim Il-sung. Kim Jong-il becomes Supreme Leader of North Korea.
- September: Release date of Windows NT 3.5.
- September: The car ferry MS Estonia sinks in the Baltic Sea, killing 852 people.
- October: Queen Elizabeth II entertained on a State visit to Russia.

- November: Sweden and Norway vote not to join the EU.
- December: Netscape Navigator Web Browser released.
- December: Release date of the PlayStation in Japan.

Zebon Copse Development Completed

The original land that the estate is built on used to be called Velmead Farm. The farm itself was part of the much larger Redfields Estate. The centrepiece of the Redfields Estate was Redfields House. The Brandon family, who owned the estate, mainly grew tobacco and hops. The hot-curing sheds, where they processed the tobacco, were situated where the Redfields Industrial Estate stands now. The estate was not split up until after the Second World War when Mr Bandon died.

The road names on the estate were chosen by Stan Knight, a resident of Crookham village, and whose family has lived in the area for many years. Brandon Road was named after the original owner of the estate whilst Blue Prior Court was named after the brand of cigarettes produced from Crookham tobacco by the firm of Stephens at Salisbury. Nicotiana Court is named after the Latin name for the tobacco plant.

CCTV Coverage Throughout Fleet

An initial system of CCTV cameras was introduced throughout Fleet Town Centre and in the wider Hart are as an initiative to reduce and deter crime. Initially set up by Hart council, the service utilised state-of-the-art analogue cameras. By 2009 technology had moved on and further investment was required to modernise the system. To save costs, monitoring of the system was shared with Rushmoor council in 2013. This arrangement lasted until recently and the current monitoring responsibility is planned to be transferred to Runnymede council. The Hart CCTV system continues to be expanded and now includes 116 Cameras.

Fleet and District U3A formed

Fleet and District U3A was formed in 1994 by a small group of interested people. U3A is an educational self-help organisation providing study groups, recreational and social activities at minimal cost. A key objective is that learning should be shared and the skills and experiences of older people should be valued. The group has attracted nearly 2000 members, with approximately 60 groups covering everything from from Art to Zumba.

Harlington Centre Opened

The Harlington Centre in Fleet has become the focus for many and varied Fleet Town community activities. Set in the heart of Fleet town, ideally placed next to the library, the site has established itself as a popular social venue and entertainment centre. It hosts a wide variety of activities and educational classes.

The site contains a number of different function rooms with different equipment and facilities available for private or company hire. The centre rose from the ashes of a major fire in 1991 and when re-opened in 1994 added a connection to the town library as well as a reception area and coffee shop.

Originally built and run by Hart District Council, The Harlington transferred into the ownership and management of Fleet Town Council in 2010.

1995

- **January:** Establishment of the World Trade Organization.
- **January:** Austria, Finland and Sweden join the European Union.
- **February:** Barings bank collapses following Nick Leeson, "Rogue Trader", loses £827m.
- **May:** Queen Elizabeth II and Queen Mother enjoyed a Royal fly past celebrating 50 years since VE Day.

- **August:** NATO bombing raids in Bosnia end the Bosnian War.

- **August:** Release date of Windows 95.
- **October:** O. J. Simpson is found not guilty of double murder for the deaths of former wife Nicole Simpson and Ronald Goldman in 1994.
- **December:** The signing of the Dayton Accords put an end to the three-and-a-half-year-long Bosnian War.

VE & VJ Day 50th Celebrations

On Monday May 8th, a large town-wide celebration for the 50th anniversary of Victory

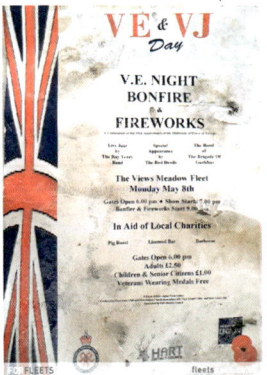

in Europe and Victory in Japan was celebrated at the Views. Organised jointly by the British Legion, Fleet Lions and Fleet Rotary the event had visitors from the sky in the form of the Army's Red Devils. The evening finished with a large firework display. Entry was free to any war veterans wearing their medals.

NGTE Transferred to DERA (Defence Evaluation and Research Agency)

In 1995 the NGTE site became part of the Defence Evaluation and Research Agency, a sub-agency of the Ministry of Defence. In 2000, due to the advent of computer simulation and testing technologies, large parts of the site were decommissioned.

Fleet Carnival Celebrates 40 years

Fleet Carnival celebrated 40 years in 1995 and the theme for the year was 'An Invitation to Party'. To celebrate the previous 40 years, the Carnival committee gathered Carnival queens from the previous 40 years and they all joined the Carnival procession in an open top bus.

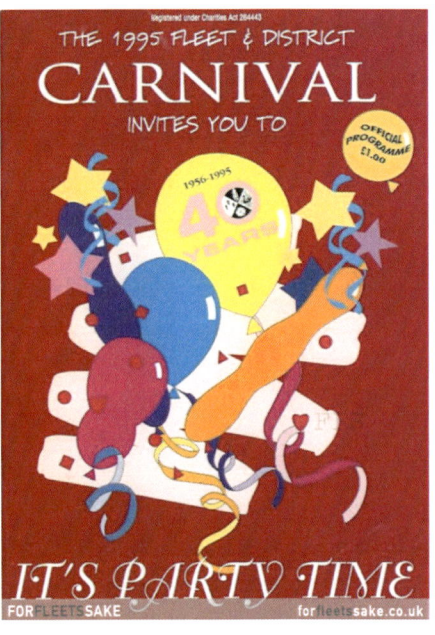

1996

- **February:** Take That, the most successful British band of the 1990s, announce that they are splitting up.
- **May:** The Duke and Duchess of York divorce, as do the Prince and Princess of Wales amid intense scrutiny from the British press.
- **June:** Release date of the Nintendo 64 video game console in Japan.
- **July:** Dolly the sheep becomes the first successfully cloned mammal.
- **July:** President Nelson Mandela of South Africa visits the UK for a State Visit.

- **August:** Release date of Windows NT 4.0.
- **August:** The First Chechen War ends.
- **September:** The Taliban government takes control of Afghanistan, creating the Islamic Emirate of Afghanistan.
- **November:** Release of DVD in Japan.

St. Nicholas School moves to Church Crookham

St Nicholas' School was founded in 1935 and first located in Branksomewood Road, Fleet, but moved to Redfields House, Church Crookham in 1996. Redfields House, a Victorian Mansion, is set in over 30 acres of glorious parkland, outdoor facilities and playing fields that all pupils get to use as often as they can.

Launch of Eagle Radio Station

Fleet's local radio station from 1996 was Eagle Radio and many of Fleet's current residents would have grown up listening to Peter Gordon and his co-host Bev. Peter Gordon began the radio station with the broadcast words "Hey I've landed" and when he eventually left in August 2020 finished with the words "After landing all those years ago, it's time for me to take off again. Thank you for listening, and for now it's cheerio".

The Old Emporium Opens as a Pub

The Emporium Pub, originally called The Old Emporium was opened as an Ale Café in 1996. This was the third in a series of Ale Café concept pubs introduced by regional brewer Greene King. It was their first pub in Fleet, they now also own the Prince of Wales.

The building dates back to the 19th century, when a James Oakley opened a general store selling everything from a bag of nails to coffins. Oakley Stores closed in 1958 and a variety of shops took over the site before it was opened as the Old Emporium.

In the 70's it was a frozen food shop and prior to opening as a pub was a Cane and Pine furniture emporium.

At the same time as the pub opened, Roger Cockram of Cockram jewellers in Fleet was commissioned to set the historic clock atop the building back into action. The regular chimes are now a familiar sound over the centre of Fleet.

1997

- **May: Tony Blair becomes Prime Minister.**
- **June: J. K. Rowling publishes Harry Potter and the Philosopher's Stone.**
- **July: The United Kingdom hands Hong Kong back to China, marking the end of the British Empire.**
- **April: The Good Friday Agreement brings an end to The Troubles in Northern Ireland.**
- **August: Princess Diana died from the injuries she sustained in a car crash in the Pont de l'Alma tunnel in Paris, France. The nation went into mourning. The following weeks represented a low point for the royal family's standing in Britain.**

- **November: the Queen and Prince Philip celebrated their golden wedding anniversary. In an anniversary speech, the Queen said: "I have done my best, with Prince Philip's constant love and help, to interpret it correctly through the years of our marriage and of my reign as your Queen. And we shall, as a family, try together to do so in the future."**

Fleet Spurs moves to Kennel Lane

Fleet Spurs Football Club, originally formed in 1948, was set up intially as a reaction or alternative to the long-established "semi-professional" Fleet Football Club. It was established with a desire to provide an amateur football club for local players combined with a strong social environment. Up until 1997, the club had played at various grounds in the Fleet area. In the 1997/8 season, they finally established a home at Kennels Lane in Southwood, part of neighbouring Rushmoor. At the same time, the first team was promoted to Hampshire League Division 2. They became champions in 1998/99 and were duly promoted to Division 1. They played two seasons in that division, finishing in sixth position, but were immediately relegated to Division 2. This was unfortunately not for football reasons, but because they failed to meet the new standards set by the league for Division 1 grounds.

Death of Yvonne Cormeau

Yvonne Cormeau, born Beatrice Yvonne Biesterfeld, was one of Fleet's bravest but least know heroes, operating as a Special Operations Executive during the Second World War. She was the second female radio operator to be sent to France.

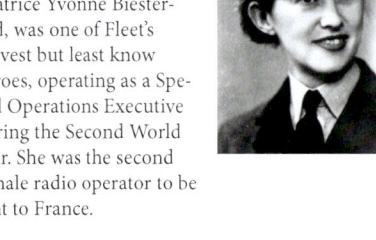

Cormeau sent over 400 transmissions back to London, which was a record for the F Section. She made arrangements for arms and supplies to be dropped for the local Maquis. She also assisted in the cutting of power and telephone lines, resulting in the isolation of the Wehrmacht Group G garrison near Toulouse. She worked for 13 months and evaded arrest despite some narrow escapes. Whilst operating in France Yvonne was shot in the leg by a German patrol, but managed to escape. The dress she wore on this occasion and the bloodstained briefcase she carried are on permanent display in the Imperial War Museum in London. After the war she was appointed MBE, and decorated with the Légion d'honneur, Croix de Guerre and Médaille de la Résistance.

Yvonne spent her later years at Tall Pines nursing home, formerly in Gally Hill Road, Fleet. Her funeral was attended by representatives from both the UK and French governments.

Harwoods Pub Opens on Fleet Road

Harwoods was a popular local pub that opened in 1997, although local opinion suggests it lost its appeal in later years.

With a dwindling customer base and with such a large building to occupy, the business closed in 2004. Prior to opening as a pub, the site had been associated with clothing and bedding, first as Longleys (1908-1974) and then as Contessa Underwear. The site is currently occupied by the Hart House pub.

Fleet Hospital Marks 100 Years of Service

It began with a meeting in 1895 at which a group of leading residents decided Fleet needed a cottage hospital. The community rallied around to raise £138 to build the new hospital. Lord Calthorpe gave the town a piece of land to build it on, on the understanding that it could only be used for health purposes or it would revert back to his ownership. The new hospital was opened on October 28th 1897 and was initially run through public subscription.

1998

- January: European Union Maastricht Treat comes into force.
- March: William, Harry and Prince Charles visited Canada on a Royal tour.

- May: Citizens of Northern Ireland and the Republic of Ireland voted in referendums on the Good Friday agreement.
- May: The Eurovision Song Contest held in Birmingham at the National Indoor Arena.
- June: The European Central Bank is formed.
- September: Google is founded by Larry Page and Sergey Brin.

- September: The Union Jack dress worn by the Spice Girl Geri Halliwell is sold at Sotheby's for £41,320.
- December: Assembly of the International Space Station commences.

Prince Arthur Pub Opens

The site now occupied by the Prince Arthur was a former plumber's merchants, Lunns, which began life as the International Grocery Shop over 100 years ago.

A large long extension to the side of the building was added when JD Wetherspoon first converted the property into the Prince Arthur pub in 1998. The pub is named after Prince Arthur, Duke of Connaught and Strathearn, Queen Victoria's third son, who lived in Fleet for five years in the 1890s when he was Commander of Aldershot Garrison.

The Prince Arthur is regularly listed in CAMRA's Good Beer Guide and offers a wide selection of real Ales. Mark Mabin and Dwayne Bailey can often be found having lunch in the pub.

Hart Football Club was founded

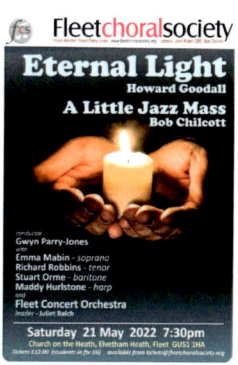

Originally know as Hart Boys FC, the club provides a safe environment for players of all abilites aged 6 to 14 to enjoy and develop their football skills.

Fleet Choral Society 20 years old

Fleet Choral Society celebrated 20 years of singing choral works in and around Fleet. Originally formed in 1967, they have remained an informal and friendly group, with over 100 members. They perform a variety of religious and secular works in three concerts per year, including an annual Christmas carol concert, that for many has become a great way to start the Christmas season. The choir has patronage from famous composers John Rutter and Bob Chilcott. It also organises regular tours to European destinations where the choir enjoy oppourtunities to perform and socialise together in interesting places.

Did you get one for Christmas?

The most popular Christmas present for 1998 was a Furby. For those who don't know, a Furby was an electroic robotic toy that resembles a hamster or owllike creature. Furbies were the first successful attempt to produce and sell a domestically-aimed robot. A newly purchased Furby starts out speaking entirely "Furbish", the unique language that all Furbies use, but is programmed to start using English words and phrases in place of Furbish over time.

1999

- **WORLD POPULATION REACHES SIX BILLION**
- **January:** Euro introduced to the financial markets. Coins and banknotes enter circulation in participating countries in 2002.
- **February:** Hugo Chavez becomes President of Venezuela.
- **May:** The Fourth Indo-Pakistani War.
- **June:** Sophie Rhys-Jones married Prince Edward at St George's Chapel, Windsor.

- **June:** The end of the Kosovo War ends the Yugoslav Wars.
- **August:** The Second Chechen War begins.
- **November:** ExxonMobil founded.
- **December:** Vladimir Putin becomes President of Russia.
- **December:** The Millennium Dome and London Eye are opened to mark the new millennium.

Rose Farm Dairy Closed

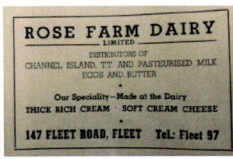

Rose Farm dairy, with their distinctive green milk floats, closed in 1999 and was transferred to the ownership of Unigate. Rose farm dairy was originally located at 147 Fleet Road. Milk deliveries in their distinctive gold and silver foil top bottles was something that generations of local people woke up to. Unfortunately, blue tits and sparrows also learned how good the freshly delivered milk was, so you would often find the bottle top pecked through and the creamy top of the milk interferred with. Wise householders would leave an old yoghourt pot to cover the top of the bottle.

1st Crookham Brownies celebrate 70 years.

Brownies, originally called Rosebuds, were first organized by Lord Baden-Powell in 1914, to complete the range of age groups for girls in Scouting. They were first run as the youngest group in the Guide Association by Agnes Baden-Powell, Lord Baden-Powell's younger sister.

Fleet in Bloom Competition Begins

The Fleet & Church Crookham in Bloom Committee, made up of representatives from appropriate voluntary organizations and Hart District Council, was formed early in 1999 with the aim of helping to enhance the appearance of our town for the new millennium.

In 1999 the Committee organized competitions for Best Shop in Fleet Road and Best Public House in Fleet & Church Crookham. Hart District Council embarked on a programme of enhancing street furniture and floral containers, together with associated improvements to the parks and open spaces in Fleet & Church Crookham. In 1999 the winner for the best shop was This "n" That Antiques and the winner of the best pub was The Wyvern.

Royal British Legion Clubhouse Closed

The Royal British Legion (RBL) Clubhouse in Fleet was closed in 1999. The Fleet, Crookham & District Branch of the RBL, is one of the oldest British Legions in the country, having been established in June 1921, just 6 weeks after the national British Legion was formed. The clubhouse was a great spot to meet up over a pint. The legion continues throughout the year to organise the local Poppy Appeal, remembrance services in Fleet and Crookham, working locally to keep profile of RBL in the minds of our community and of course organising some great social events.

2000

- **January:** The first day of the 3rd millennium is celebrated worldwide on New Year's Day. The Queen opens various landmarks including the Millenium Bridge.

- **February:** A rare century leap year date occurs.
- **March:** The Sony PlayStation 2 releases in Japan.
- **May:** The ILOVEYOU computer virus affects Windows computers and spreads fast.
- **May:** India becomes the second country to reach 1 billion people.
- **November:** George W. Bush is elected President of the United States, after a contentious recount in Florida.
- **November:** First long-term residents of the International Space Station, whose first component was launched in 1998.

Gurkas Leave Fleet and Crookham

Gurkhas were stationed at Queen Elizabeth Barracks, Church Crookham for 29 years (1971-2000). They were much admired by local residents for their excellent discipline, friendly nature and smart appearance. In August 2000 they sadly had to leave Fleet and are now based at Shorncliffe, Folkestone, Kent. On 5 August 2000, the 1st Battalion of the Gurkha Rifles, marched down Fleet Road to say goodbye to the community. The Gurkhas presented a gift to the people of Fleet, which is a painting that hangs in the entrance to the Harlington.

A Gurkha Statue has been given as an important memorial to the people of Church Crookham and Fleet, as well as to those Gurkhas and their families who travel to see it as an act of both remembrance and celebration. The Gurkha statue was unveiled in Church Crookham on 10th July 2016 in the Sirmoor memorial gardens.

Fleet Coaches sold to Truemans

Fleet Coaches was founded in 1946 and sold in 2000 to Truemans Travel of Deepcut when the owners took retirement. Fleet Coaches were a daily sight throughout the area running short holidays, school runs and charter operations extensively throughout the 1970s, 80s and 90s.

They were a typical small independent family run coach firm operating local contracts and UK & Continental tours. In total the firm owned 82 coaches of which the average fleet size was approximately 12. Their livery was an attractive two-tone blue.

Elvetham Heath Construction begins with removal of old railway bridge

Elvetham Heath is a major development and suburb of Fleet on the land that was previously known as Railway Heath. The development consists of 2000 homes and has a population of 5183 people. Work began on the development in the summer of 1999, and ended in June 2008.

Lee Biggins, Local Entrepreneur starts CV Library

Lee Biggins, local entrepreneur and owner of

CV-Library began his business with founding partner Brian Wakem in 2000. According the Sunday Times Rich List in 2019 Lee Biggins, who has also expanded into the US with Resume-Library, is now worth in excess of £150m. Biggins was quoted in 1999 as saying "in school I was pretty disruptive; acting the class clown, distracting people. I had no interest in learning and teachers couldn't get through to me. I used to dread parents' evenings".

Shotts Nightclub Burns Down

Shotts Nightclub, on the site of the previous Peter Driver Sports centre, burnt down in mysterious circumstances in June 2000. Bourley Grange care home now stands on the old Shotts site.

2001

- **June:** Eleven members of the royal family of Nepal, including the king and queen, are killed by Crown Prince Dipendra, who wounds himself and dies three days later.

- **September 11 attacks:** Al-Qaeda terrorists hijack four planes, crashing two into the twin towers of the World Trade Center in New York City, the third plane into the Pentagon in Washington, DC, while the fourth plane is downed on the outskirts of Stonycreek Township, Pennsylvania. 2,996 people, including 2,977 victims and 19 hijackers, die in the attacks.

- **October:** The United States invades Afghanistan and topples the Taliban regime, resulting in a long-term war.

- **October:** Steve Jobs introduces the first iPod.

- **December:** Enron files for Chapter 11 bankruptcy after a series of scandals.

- **December:** During an economic crisis in Argentina, the government effectively freezes all bank accounts for twelve months which leads to riots and President de la Rúa's resignation from office. There are five presidents in less than a month.

Map of developments in Fleet in the 2000's overlaid on 1950s OS Map. Note previous developments from 1950s to 1990s are shaded in blue

Fleet Medical Centre Opened

Fleet Medical Centre, originally costing £820,000 was opened by local MP James Arbuthnot in May 2001. The medical centre is in the grounds of Fleet Hospital in Church Road Fleet. Previously the Medical practice had been operating out of Burnside Surgery in Connault Road. The two-storey building, which began serving patients in January, includes a dental suite, pharmacy and a health education room. Dr. Rolan Aubrey was the senior partner at the time. Dr. Aubrey is the father of famous fleet actress Juliet Aubrey.

Fleet Motor Club

Fleet Motor Club was formed in August 2001 and has grown to attract 200 regular drivers. The club was an idea and lifelong dream of Colin Roberts "Head of the Roberts family". His seven children have all been raised with Motor Racing in their blood, which has proved to be an added inspiration in the creation of what family and friends worked so hard toward.

Fleet Town Girls Football Club Formed

The girls club began in 2001, the Ladies Adult section was formed in 2009 as a natural progression for players from Fleet Town Girls. As of 2018 the club was the largest all girls football club in Hampshire, providing high quality football to more that 150 players from Fleet and the surrounding area.

Noel Edmonds at Courtmoor

As part of Noel's House Party, Noel Edmonds once flew in by helicopter to Court Moor school to Gunge the Head Master, Mr Ken Shorey. Quite a surprise for the pupils of the school at the time but even more of a surprise for Mr Shorey.

2002

- January: The Euro enters circulation.
- January: The Guantanamo Bay detention camp is established.
- February: Princess Margaret dies aged 71.
- March: The Queen Mother dies aged 101.
- March: SpaceX is founded by Elon Musk.
- May: East Timor gains independence.
- June: The Queen celebrates her Golden Jubilee.

- July: The International Criminal Court is established.
- July: The African Union is founded.
- September: Mozilla Firefox is released.
- November: The 2002-2004 SARS outbreak begins in Guangdong.

Christmas Tree Decorating

The annual Christmas Tree decorating festival begins at St. Philip and St. James Church. This annual event attracts entrants from businesses, community groups, schools and individuals from across the town. Visitors to the festival vote on their favourite treas, while enjoying music from local performers.

Dakotas Pub Closed

Dakotas pub restaurant was closed and the complete restaurant and pub was refurbished to become the Heron on the Lake, which opened in 2003.

Byrne Brothers Closed

Ray Byrne, the last in a line of Byrne brothers to run the iconic Byrne Brothers newsagent in Beacon Hill Road, retired in January 2002. The Byrne Brothers newsagent still stands closed up, looking very much as it did when it closed in 2002. Bill was the third generation of Byrnes to run the newsagents. His father, also called Bill Byrne, and his grandmother Florence Byrne had all run the newsagents before him. Bill's mother Delia Byrne was a familiar face in the family shop, continuing to work until she was 94. By the time the shop closed in 2002 it had served the Crookham Crossroads area for 80 years.

Gurkka Camp development commenced at Queen Elizabeth Barracks.

Bryant Homes, part of Taylor Woodrow, purchased the old Gurkha camp at Church Crookham with a view to building 1,100 new homes by 2004. Initially the development was to be called Khukri Park, in honour of its Gurkha heritage, but this ultimately became Crookham Park. In an interesting planning observation, the release of this land removed the immediate need to develop houses along Hitches Lane, as this new development would meet all of the districts housing requirements until 2006. As all the residents of Fleet know, Hitches Lane came back as a site for development within just a few years as the site of Edenbrook.

2003

- **February:** Space Shuttle Columbia disintegrates upon reentry, killing all 7 astronauts on board.
- **March:** The United Kingdom, alongside the US, invades Iraq.
- **April:** The Human Genome Project is completed.
- **August:** Ronaldo makes his debut for Manchester United.

- **August:** The highest temperature ever recorded in the UK - 38.5°C (101.3°F) at Brogdale near Faversham in Kent.
- **November:** Final flight of the SST (Supersonic Transport) Concorde.

- **December:** Queen Elizabeth II and the Duke of Ediburgh visited Nigeria and opened the Commonwealth heads of Government meeting.

United Reformed Church Modernised

The United Reformed Church premises began extensive modernisation, adding a new hall, kitchen, meeting rooms, office and vestibule This modernisation was, from the outset, for the mutual benefit of the members of the church and the local community, and the buildings continue to be widely used by a variety of community organisations. These were completed in 2004.

Breaking Records

Fleet's Graeme Pullen claimed what was thought to be a national record catch of Carp on floaters. He fished with mate Ted Kershaw at Lake Farm near Aldershot. They netted 117 carp in an 11 hour daytime session. The largest fish was 14lbs caught by Graeme.

Derek Hayes 80th Birthday

Long term resident and owner of Hayes & Son shoe shop in Reading Road South celebrated his 80th birthday and his 67th year serving in the shop. The shop opened in the 1920's and unfortunately had to close in 2016.

Fleet Pond Society Awarded Queens Golden Jubilee Award

Fleet Pond Society works in partnership with Hart District Council to conserve the fabulous community asset that is Fleet Pond Nature Reserve. In 2003 the Fleet Pond Society was awarded the Queen's Golden Jubilee Award for Voluntary Service. The award read "For the outstanding work they do in promoting, preserving and maintaining the Fleet Pond Nature Reserve and promoting its use as a public amenity and a Site of Special Interest, the Fleet Pond Society have been awarded the Queen's Golden Jubilee Award for Voluntary Service by groups in the community for 2003."

First Fleet Christmas Festival

In a concerted effort to bring the local community together at the beginning of Christmas, Fleet Town Business Community began the now landmark Fleet Christmas Festival and lights switch on.

A life sized replica of the Whittle jet plane

The replica Jet was officially unveiled by Sir Ralph Robbins. Roy Fowkes, a friend of Sir Frank Whittle, headed a group that raised £80,000 to build the replica.

2004

- **January:** Spirit and Opportunity land on Mars.

- **February:** Facebook is formed by Mark Zuckerberg, Andrew McCollum, Eduardo Saverin, Dustin Moskovitz, and Chris Hughes.

- **May:** NATO and the European Union incorporates most of the former Eastern Bloc.
- **June:** The 60th anniversary of D-Day is remembered by world leaders.
- **July:** First surface images of Saturn's moon Titan.
- **November:** Orange Revolution in Ukraine.
- **November:** President of the Palestinian National Authority Yasser Arafat dies.
- **December:** Boxing Day Tsunami occurs in Indian Ocean, leading to the deaths of 230,000.
- **December:** Fox hunting was outlawed in the UK.

Helen Reeves wins Bronze Medal in K1 Kayaking Athens Olympics

Helen Reeves, born in 1980 in Fleet, won a bronze medal in the K1 Kayak class at the Athens Summer Olympics in 2004. Helen, a former Heatherside School pupil, tried slalom for the first time on the Basingstoke Canal at Fleet Wharf.

North Hants Golf Club Centenary

North Hants Golf Club was an ambitious project when it was opened in 1904 by Princess Alexander of Teck. It offered the ethos of a

gentleman's club to attract members from London and the atmosphere of an American Country Club with, in addition to a fine golf course, lawn tennis courts and croquet lawns of the highest quality.

The Golf course was originally designed by James Braid, extensively redesigned in 1913 by Harry Colt and further improved in 1930 by Tom Simpson. More recently, three new holes were designed by Donald Steel in 2001 and a magnificent new clubhouse was opened in 2003. The Centenary was celebrated on 6th May 2004, exactly 100 years to the day of the opening ceremony of the course.

Safeway's becomes Morrisons

The Safeway supermarket on Elvetham Heath was rebranded as Morrisons, following Morrisons' £3bn takeover of the Safeway supermarket chain in March 2004.

Crookham Infants Expands

Crookham Infants School received £500,000 worth of investment which provided for two new classrooms, bringing all the children under one roof.

Justin Rose MBE Leaves Fleet for Florida

Justin Rose was born in Johannesburg, South Africa, to English parents, Annie and Ken. The family moved to Fleet when Rose was five, and he started to play golf at Tylney Park Golf Club. He then moved on to Southwood Golf Club, Hartley Wintney Golf Club, and finally North Hants Golf Club. Fleet's Olympic gold medal winner was also honoured with an MBE for his services to golf in 2017.

2005

YouTube — Broadcast Yourself™

- **February:** YouTube is founded by Jawed Karim, Chad Hurley and Steve Chen.
- **April:** MG Rover goes bust.
- **April:** Prince Charles married Camilla Parker Bowles.

- **May:** Tony Blair elected for third term.
- **July:** The Irish Republican Army announces it is officially ending its violent campaign for a united Ireland and will instead pursue its goals politically.
- **July:** 7/7 attacks on London Underground.
- **November:** Angela Merkel becomes Germany's first female Chancellor.

Propaganda Music Canteen Opens

The Hogshead Pub in Fleet Road was transformed in 2005 into the Propaganda Music Canteen.

Elvetham Road Cleared of Speed Limiting Measures

Chicanery at Elvetham Road was removed at cost of £30,000. In one of the most contentious local road calming schemes, public opinion finally won over and the speed limiting bumps and chicanes that had been installed in Elvetham Road only the year before were removed. The speed limiting measures had caused numerous damage to cars and were a source of significant road noise.

Old Skatepark Removed and Improved

The old skateboard park on the Views was completely removed to make way for the new road link between Victoria Rd car park and Harlington Way. It was replaced by a larger much improved version pictured below.

New Footbridge joining Elvetham Heath to Fleet Opened.

A new footbridge which links Elvetham Heath estate with Elvetham Heath Rd provided much improved access to Fleet Town Centre and Fleet Railway station for walkers and cyclists living on the estate.

Fleet Athlete wins 100m Gold Medal

Fleet athlete Vicki Hansfords won the 100m gold medal in the Wheelchair and Amputee World Games at Rio de Janeiro.

2006

April: Queen's 80th birthday

- **March: Twitter is launched.**
- **August: The International Astronomical Union creates the first formal definition of a planet, and excludes Pluto from the list.**
- **October: Google acquires YouTube for US$1.65 billion.**
- **November: Former Russian security agent Alexander Litvinenko dies from poisoning in the UK.**
- **November: Nintendo launches the Wii.**

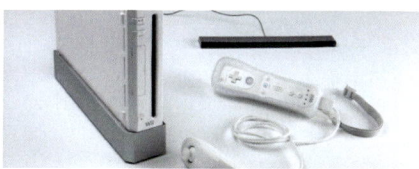

Fleet Angler Graeme Pullen Catches Record Porbeagle Shark.

Fleet celebrity angler Graeme Pullen and his friend Peter Scott caught the biggest Porbeagle shark ever landed in the UK. It weighed 550lb and was caught of the coast of Bude in Cornwall. He was up to his tricks again in 2014, catching a similar sized monster.

Church on the Heath Opens

A joint project to open a church that was built embracing Anglican, Baptist, Methodist and United Reformed traditions. The Church was planted in the centre of the Elvetham Heath development, built on land kindly donated for this specific purpose. It has become a vibrant centre enjoyed by many members of the local community.

Fleet Boys Live Longer

According to the office of National Statistics, Fleet boys born in 2006 should look forwards to living until they 80 - up to 4 years longer than those born in other parts of the country.

Fleet Football Player signs for Fulham

Fleet youngster Neil Etheridge signed as a goal keeper at the age of 16 for Fulham Football Club. Neil has gone on to play with Oldham, in the premiership with Cardiff City and most recently in the championship with Birmingham. He has been capped multiple times for the Phillipines national team.

2007

- **May: Disappearance of Madeleine McCann.**
- **June: Introduction of the iPhone by Apple.**
- **June: Gordon Brown becomes Prime Minister.**
- **October: Airbus A380 Begins commercial flights with Singapore Airlines.**
- **November: Queen and Prince Philip's Diamond wedding anniversary.**

- **December: Spike in food prices and subprime crisis help trigger global recession.**

Fleet Angels begins serving the Night time community of Fleet

Fleet Angels, a group of volunteers who are present on the streets of Fleet during the late night hours on Friday and Saturday, began their helpful and much appreciated work. An initiative of the local Churches, Fleet Angels were originally called the Fleet Town Centre Project and were established to provide a safe place and support for anyone in the town late at night. Most often these are youngsters who perhaps have drunk too much, but also they have provided support to the homeless, troubled youngsters, and those who work in the town at night including door staff, restaurant staff and taxi drivers. Fleet Angel's calming and supportive presence has ensured many have gotten home safely, and bought calm and reason into many disputes that might otherwise have escalated. They are known for the flip flops. lollipos, hot drinks and biscuits that they provide.

Fleet Scout Troop Celebrates 80th Birthday

Fleet Scouts has a long history. In 2007 the 22nd Odiham troop celebrated 80 years in Fleet.

Cattle introduced to Velmead Common

A bull, two calves and four cows were introduced to Velmead Common as part of the Hampshire Wildlife Trust's Grazing for Biodiversity Project. The intention was to rejuvenate neglected heathland.

Fleet Lions First Beer Festival

Fleet Lions first Beer festival was held in August 2007. This has now become an annual event in the Fleet calendar.

Pondtail Post Office Closed in Kings Road

Pondtail Post Office, which had been open in the same spot since 1910, was forced to close as a result of a government initiaitve closing 2,500 regional Post Offices. The shop tried to remain open as a corner shop, but eventually closed in 2012 after which it was converted into flats.

CountryWide Buses Change Name to Fleet Buzz

The memorable Fleet Buzz buses first begain serving the streets of Fleet using their new name in 2007.

2008

- **February: Tesla Roadster launched - the first mass production lithium-ion battery electric car.**

- **February: Prince Harry was brought home from Afganistan after serving secretly for two months, following fears for his safety after a leak to the press.**

- **September: Stock markets plunge around the world, signaling the start of the Great Recession.**

- **September: The Large Hadron Collider is completed as the world's largest and most powerful particle collider.**

- **November: Barack Obama is elected to become the first black President of the United States.**

Fleet and Crookham Local History Group Given Lottery Grant

Fleet and Crookham Local History Group successfully bid for a National Lottery Grant to help protect, improve access to, and publicise, local history.

Geoff Baker Honoured with Award at Bakers' 100th Anniversary

Fleet Lions made Geoff Baker from WC

Bakers a Melvin Jones Fellow. Geoff has sponsored many activities in Fleet including Fleet Carnival and Festivities. His family shop opened in 1908, and the whole town was saddened when it needed to close in 2021.

Avondale Tennis Club celebrated its 100th Anniversary

Avondale Lawn Tennis Club first began in 1908 and celebrated 100 years in 2008 with a display of photographs and memorabilia at Fleet Library. It began life as a cycle club. In 2008 there were 400 members and 200 juniors.

Crookham Village celebrates 25 years of being twinned with Levignen

Crookham Village and Levignen in Picardy have celebrated 25 years of twinning. More than 40 people from Church Crookham travelled to France to celebrate with a dinner and dance and renewal of the twinning charter, originally signed in 1983. Recognising the deep connections between the two villages, Levignen has named various buildings after their twins in Crookham Village and Crookham Village has a Levingnen Close as part of Zebon Copse developments.

Elvetham Heath Completed

The final house in the Elvetham Heath development was built in 2008, marking another significant expansion of the Fleet housing footprint.

2009

- **January:** Chesley Sullenberger lands the US Airways Flight no. 1549 on the Husdon river, ensuring all passengers survived.
- **January:** The cryptocurrency Bitcoin is launched.
- **March:** Albania and Croatia join NATO.
- **April:** Barack and Michelle Obama visit with the Queen and a hug is caught on camera.

- **May:** NASA launches the final space shuttle mission to the Hubble Telescope.
- **June:** Swine flu pandemic began in North America.
- **June:** Michael Jackson dies of cardiac arrest in Los Angeles aged 50.

Dean and Alison Give Birth to Twins Twice

Dean Durrant and Alison Spooner, a Fleet couple, made it into the Guinness Book of Records when they gave birth to a second set of twins in December 2008. Dean and Alison, who are a mixed race couple, had given birth a second time to biracial twins, where one of the pair was black and the other white. When it first happened in 2001 it was considered extremely rare, so when it happened a second time in 2008 it was considered so rare that they made into the Guinness Book of Records.

Fleet Remembrance Parade Re-introduced

For the first time in over a decade, Fleet and Church Crookham commemorated Remembrance Sunday with a parade which started from Church Rd car park after a remembrance service at All Saints Church. The parade ended in Gurkha Square where the service was continued with the laying of wreaths at the War Memorial by the Chairman of Hart DC, local MP James Arbuthnot and other local groups and organisations. The parade was organised by the Fleet, Crookham & District Branch of the Royal British Legion. The annual remembrance parade has become an increasingly important part of bringing together the community in Fleet and Church Crookham.

Lions Community Store wins Sainsburys Charity of the Year

The Lions Community store was voted Sainsbury's charity of the year in 2009. The store, founded in 1995, had handed out furniture and household items to more than 45,000 people at the time of the award in 2009. It continues to operate providing a much needed service to those in need of good quality donated furniture. During the 2020-2021 Covid pandemic, it served a much needed role providing laptop computers to local school children and vulnerable adults.

Fleet News and Fleet Mail newspapers join to create Fleet News and Mail

The Fleet News and The Fleet Mail merged together to produce one broadsheet which was published every Friday. The Fleet News was founded in 1894 providing news in Fleet and the surrounding community. The title was taken over by the national publisher Reach, who no longer publish a physical local newspaper, instead offering a digital version.

6 Inches of Snow Feb 2009

Families woke to heavy snow in February 2009.

2010

- March: Moscow Metro bombings.
- April: The iPad is introduced.
- April: The largest oil spill in US history occurs in the Gulf of Mexico.
- May: David Cameron becomes Prime Minister.
- October: Instagram is launched.
- November: The threat of Greece defaulting on its debts triggers the European sovereign debt crisis and Republic of Ireland's financial crisis.
- December: Arab Spring starts.
- December: The queen becomes a great-grandmother when Savannah Phillips is born.

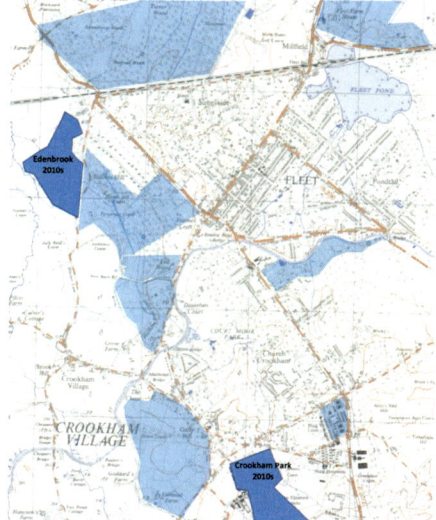

Map of developments in Fleet in the 2010's overlaid on 1950s OS Map. Note previous developments from 1950s to 2000s are shaded in blue

Wrights the Bakery closed

D.R. Wrights and Sons bakery, which had served Fleet since 1936, closed. The shop is now occupied by Serendipity, but still retains the distinctive Hovis sign above the upper floor windows. Wrights bakers closed in 2008 after serving Fleet faithfully for 50 years. Local people will have fond memories of the pastries, flap jacks, apple puffs and bread puddings that were a distinctive part of the home-baked experience that the Wrights bought to Fleet Road.

In 2012 Mrs. Shillings took over the lease on the shop. She called the shop Serendipity and sold gifts and ran a tea shop at the back where the bread used to be baked. Mrs Shillings kept the iconic Hovis sign on the front of the shop, but removed the bread ovens.

Monster Raving Looney Party Confernece Held in Fleet

Alan "Howling Laud" Hope is a famous resident of Fleet and as leader of the Monster Raving Looney Party has organised many annual conferences around the area. Most memorable to Fleet was the one in 2010, when the special guest star and visitor was Adam Ant. The conference was held in the Links Pub, now known as the Station Hotel. Alan recalls "He bought a guitarist with him and sang all his hits. He brought the place to its knees".

Monster Raving Looney party leader Alan "Howling Laud" Hope was returned unopposed as the parish councillor for the Fleet Central Ward in 2010. Only four people put their names forward for the five seats.

Exchequer Pub Re-launched in Crookham Village

Tom and Vicki Faulkner breathed new life into the old Chequers pub in Crookham Village, by refurbishing and focussing on quality food utilising the best local suppliers. In 2010 they renamed the pub "The Exchequer", a play on the name Ex-Chequers. The pub has gone on to establish an excellent reputation and is currently part of the Red Mist Leisure group that has sought to breathe new life into pubs throughout the local area.

Creation of Fleet Town Council along with Elvetham Heath Parish Council and Church Crookham Parish Council.

2011

- **WORLD POPULATION REACHES SEVEN BILLION.**
- **April:** The world watched as Prince William married Kate Middleton at Westminster Abbey in a fairytale wedding. The Queen makes an official visit to Ireland for the first time.

- **May:** Osama bin Laden is shot dead by United States Navy SEALs in Pakistan.
- **July:** Snapchat launched.
- **August:** Space Shuttle program is officially ended.
- **August:** NASA launches Juno spacecraft to visit Jupiter and Mars.
- **October:** Apple Co-founder Steve Jobs dies aged 56.
- **December:** Iraq War ends.

Fleet Phoenix Opens Doors at the Point

Fleet Phoenix grew out of an initiative to host a youth café, that originally began as a trial in 2010. The café became a success providing a safe space for teenagers to visit on a Friday evening. This initiative grew into the establishment of Fleet Phoenix that currently serves various projects engaged with encouraging and helping youth throughout the town.

New Play Area Opened at Ancell's Farm

Fleet Town Council chairman Bob Schofield

opened a new £60,000 children's play area at Ancells Farm. This was added to by the local residents, the friends of Ancells farm and a government grant. The childrens play equipment has now been significantly upgraded and in 2021 a concrete table tennis table was donated by Court Moor School.

Hart Foodbank Opens in Fleet

In 2011 a Foodbank was launched in Hart. Food is collected from individuals and organisations and vouchers issued by doctors, social services, job centres and churches to those most in need. The Foodbank operates out of four locations throughout Hart, including the Methodist Church in Fleet. The Foodbank is now part of the nationwide Trussel Trust helping the most vulnerable and needy in our society.

Phyllis Tuckwells Shop Re-opened by Raquel Cassidy

Fleet's Phyllis Tuckwell was re-opened by famous local actress Raquel Cassidy following a fire early in the year. Phyllis Tuckwell operate 18 charity shops throughout the local area supporting the hospice which opened in 1979. They are world leaders in end of life care.

Redfields Garden Centre starts renovation

Redfields is one of the oldest garden centres in the country and in 2010 it was sold for redeveloped to its new owners the Blue Diamond Group. Previous owners Malcolm and Anne Goater had run the Redfield's Garden Centre for the last 32 years as a local family business. Final redevelopment was completed in 2014. In 2016 it was awarded the prestigious Horticulture Week's Best Business Development Award.

2012

- **March:** The US rover, Curiosity, takes a selfie on Mars and finds evidence of an ancient streambed of water on the Red Planet.
- **March:** The Shard tops out in construction, becoming the tallest building in Western Europe.
- **June:** The Queen marks her Diamond Jubilee.

- **June:** The Queen made a cameo performance alongside Daniel Craig as James Bond for the opening of the London 2012 Olympics. In a short parody film, Bond actor Daniel Craig entered Buckingham Palace wearing his trademark tuxedo. After a pause, Her Majesty turns from her writing desk and says simply: 'Good evening, Mr. Bond.'
- **July:** The Higgs boson is discovered.
- **October:** Skydiver Felix Baumgartner becomes the first person to break the sound barrier without a vehicle.
- **November:** Xi Jinping is elected as General Secretary of the Chinese Communist Party.

Fleet's Lucy Shuker wins Bronze in London Olympics

Lucy Shuker, who grew up in Fleet, is a British wheelchair tennis player who is currently the highest ranked woman in the sport in Britain. Lucy has represented Great Britain at three successive Paralympic Games, twice winning a bronze medal in the women's doubles and is former World Doubles Champion and World Team Cup Silver Medallist amongst a number of other National and International successes. Lucy made history at the London 2012 Paralympics alongside fellow Brit Jordanne Whiley when the pair became the first women to win a medal for Great Britain in wheelchair tennis, coming from match point down to secure Bronze in the women's doubles event.

Jazz club launched

Fleet Jazz Club was launched in the Harlington Centre on Jan 15 2012. It is held on the third Tuesday of each month and brings the best of national jazz talent into the centre of Fleet.

Best of British

Hart was selected as the best place to live in by an Halifax quality of life survey. Hart gained first place after two years as runner up to Elmbridge.
The study by the Halifax bank took into account factors such as jobs, housing, health, life expectancy, crime, weather, traffic and house prices.

Jubilee Wood Opened at Calthorpe Park

To commemorate the Queen's Diamond Jubilee in 2012, the Friends of Calthorpe Park helped plant a 15 tree Jubilee Wood in Calthorpe Park. This is located next to the wooden swan structure and also has two park benches so people can sit and relax in the area whilst walking through Calthorpe Park.

Ken Heanes Passed away

Former England motorcycle manager Ken Heanes, known as the Fleet Flyer, died at his home in Winchfield. Ken was a leading figure in the world of motorcycling, initially as a competitor, then as a motorcycle designer and laterly as a retailer with a large iconic motorcycle shop in Reading Road South. He was a good friend of Steve McQueen, who was known to visit him in Fleet in preparation for the making of the film "The Great Escape". Ken Heanes designed the bike modifications to the motorbike used by McQueen in the jump scenes of the film.

2013

- **January:** Horse meat was found in burgers being sold in some supermarkets.
- **February:** Pope Benedict XVI resigns, the first Pope to do since 1415, and Pope Francis is elected, becoming the first Pope from Latin America.
- **April:** Death and funeral of Margaret Thatcher.

- **May:** Edward Snowden releases classified documents concerning mass surveillance by the NSA.
- **July:** Same-sex marriage is legalized in the United Kingdom.
- **July:** The Duke and Duchess of Cambridge welcomed their first child, Prince George, on 22nd July 2013.

- **December:** Death and state funeral of Nelson Mandela at the age of 95.

Guides Community Hall Opens

In February 2013 the old Guide division HQ was demolished and work on a built-to-purpose Headquarters commenced. Work was finished by Sept 2013 and all guiding units moved back into the Headquarters. In 2022 Fleet division, covering Fleet, Church Crookham, Crookham village, Dogmersfield and Crondall has 27 units and over 700 members.

British Bake-off Semi-finalist

31 year old Beca Lyne-Pirkis from Church Crookham reached the semi finals of the British Bake Off BBC programme.

John Pinkerton II launched

Following the retirement of the original John Pinkerton canal boat in 2012, the John Pinkerton II was launched in July 2013. In the naming ceremony Sally Taylor of BBC South Today was given the honour of pouring champagne over her bow.

Justin Rose wins US Open

Fleet's Justin Rose, who is a member of the North Hants Golf Club, has become the first Englishman to win the US Open in 43 years.

Fleet Food Festival

2013 was the first year for Fleet's annual Food Festival. The amazing food markets celebrate the best in food and drink, including specialist food, live music and entertainment.

2014

- **February:** Euromaidan protest in Ukraine sparks a revolution and the overthrow of Viktor Yanukovych, leading to Russia's annexation of Crimea and war in the Donbas.
- **March:** The worst Ebola epidemic in recorded history occurs in West Africa, infecting nearly 30,000 people and resulting in the deaths of 11,000+.

- **April:** Photograph commissioned to celebrate Queen's 88th birthday.
- **May:** Narendra Modi is elected as the Prime Minister of India.
- **June:** ISIS begins its offensive in northern Iraq, leading to intervention in Iraq and Syria by a US-led coalition.
- **September:** The Scottish independence referendum takes place; Scotland decides to remain part of the United Kingdom.

- **November:** The Rosetta spacecraft's Philae probe becomes the first to successfully land on a comet.

Fleet listed in The Best Places to Live Survey

According to the Times in March 2014 - "Several studies have found the residents of Hart, in the northeastern corner of wealthy Hampshire, known for its wooded landscape and freshwater lake and centred around the picturesque town of Fleet, to be some of the happiest in the UK and live the longest. They pay for that privilege with house prices significantly higher than the national average."

New Tweseldown Infant School Built

The new school Tweseldown Infants scchool was built in 2014 and is set in extensive grounds. The school benefits from a large field, a shade hut, hard surfaced playground, a wildlife area and an adventure playground.

Local girl Isobel Pooley wins silver medal in Commonwealth Games

In June 2014 Isobel Pooley won the High Jump in the UK Championships with a height of 1.90m. In August she went on to win a silver medal at the Commonwealth Games in Glasgow, with a new best of 1.92m. Three weeks later, she broke the UK outdoor record, when she improved her best by 4 cm to 1.96m in Eberstadt, Germany. The previous UK record of 1.95m had first been set by Diana Davies (then Elliott) in 1982. It was then equalled in 2001 by Susan Moncrieff and again in 2007 by Olympic Heptathlon Champion Jessica Ennis, before Pooley finally surpassed it. The record was one of the longest standing UK outdoor field event records.

Improvements at Fleet Station

The 1960s Fleet Station was replaced and a deck added to the southern car park adjacent to Fleet Pond to provide extra spaces.

Fleet Police Station Closes

The decision to close Fleet police station was made in 2011 in an attempt to save £50 million by 2015. The actual closure took place in 2014. The building was finally sold for redevelopment in 2019 for a price of £1,342,974. It is currently being redeveloped into 31 apartments.

M3 Transition to Smart Motorway

Work to convert the M3 into a Smart Motorway commenced in October 2014. Originally planned to be completed within 2 years, the plans overran and the conversion was not finished until 2017.

2015

- **September:** Queen Elizabeth II became the longest-reigning British monarch on 9th September 2015, surpassing the reign of her great great grand mother Victoria. The Queen had been reigning for more than 63 years. On May 2nd Princess Charlotte of Cambridge is born.

- **September:** Liquid water is found on Mars.

- **September:** Volkswagen emissions scandal was acknowledged when VW admitted they had installed "defeat devices".

- **December:** China announces the end of One Child Policy after 35 years.

- **December:** Tim Peake becomes the first British ESA astronaut to board the International Space Station.

Ancient Roman Building Foundations Discovered at Hitches Farm.

An archeological investigation was initially carried out on the site now occupied by the Edenbrook development in 2007-2008. More detailed excavations were carried out by Thames Valley Archaeological Services who undertook further excavations at Hitches Farm discovering evidence of both Bronze Age and Roman activity at the farm site. The foundations of a large rectangular timber building were uncovered together with over 300 shards of Roman Pottery and coins dating from the 2nd Century.

All Saints Church Burned Down

On 16 June 2015 a 17 year old set fire to a Bible at All Saints Church, but little damage was done. He returned on 22 June and sprayed the shape of a cross with a deodorant can on a wall near the altar before igniting it and making off. An estimated £4.5m of damage was caused in the resulting major fire. Restoration is now well under way.

Ant and Dec Visit

Fleet went Ant and Dec crazy when the celebrity duo made a surprise visit to the town to officially unveil its new Paddington Bear statue in 2015.

There were excited screams from children and parents as the Geordie presenters made a surprise entrance on The Harlington stage to reveal Bear Humbug, one of 50 specially designed statues dotted around London to celebrate the Paddington movie launch in November 2015.

Fleet Town Football Club was 125 Years Old

Fleet Town FC was officially formed in 1890, making it the oldest sports club in the town. The centenary was celebrated in 1990 with a special scroll being presented by the Football Association to the club, together with a commemorative plaque from the Hampshire FA. In its early years Fleet FC played at the bottom of the Views where Campbells Close is today. Later they moved to Watsons Meadow in Fleet Road, roughly opposite where Travis & Perkins now stands, at the station end of Fleet Road. It was during this time that a young, future Prime Minister, Clement Atlee played for the club, his aunt living in a house that backed onto this original ground.

2016

- **April:** The queen celebrates her 90th birthday. She also becomes the world's longest-reigning, still-serving monarch after the death of the king of Thailand. Celebrations included street parties across the country, celebrity performances and a flypast from the balcony of Buckingham Palace during Trooping the Colour.
- **April:** Panama Papers, a leak of legal documents, reveals information of 214,888 offshore companies.
- **June:** The Gotthard Base Tunnel, the world's longest and deepest railway tunnel, is completed.
- **June:** The people of the United Kingdom vote to leave the European Union; David Cameron resigns.
- **July:** Theresa May becomes the second female Prime Minister of the United Kingdom.
- **August:** Great Britain ranks second on the 2016 Summer Olympics medal table with 27 Gold Medals, the best result since 1908.
- **September:** Mother Teresa is officially canonized by Pope Francis.
- **November:** Donald Trump wins the 2016 presidential election, in an upset against Hillary Clinton, the first female to be nominated for a major party.

Fleet Lions Take Delivery of new Santa Sleigh

Fleet Lions have been a familiar sight in and around Fleet at Christmas through their Santa sleigh. Over the years they have collected a considerable amount of money that has been given to local deserving projects. In December 2016 they upgraded their sleigh to a new version kindly manufactured for them by Cove Industries.

Biggest Fireball caught on camera in Church Crookham

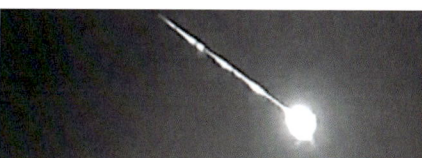

One of the biggest fireballs ever recorded by amateur astronomers in Britain was caught on camera in Church Crookham in March 2016.

The meteor was spotted at about 3.16am and as it passed the Earth's atmosphere and heated up it emitted a light almost as bright as a full moon. It was so vivid that the meteor's flash of light, which lasted only a few seconds, lit up the whole sky. The UK Meteor Network, set up in 2012, captured the fireball on eight of its cameras.

This was the biggest one ever recorded by the Meteor Network. It was first recorded in Church Crookham.

High Fleet Life Expectancy

Men in Fleet North ward are revealed to have the second highest life expectancy in England and Wales.

According to a Lancet publication in November 2016, men in the Fleet North ward had a life expectancy of 89.7 years, compared to the national average of 79.3.

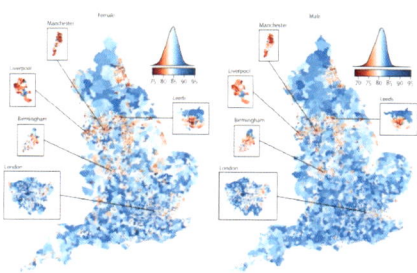

Chainsaw Carving in Gurkha Square

Hart District Council and Fleet Town Council commissioned chainsaw artist Rob Beckinsale to convert an old dead tree in Gurkha Square to a magnificent carving which highlights the various activities offered by the Harlington Centre and the Library.

The carving was part of the councils environmental enhancement projects, with funding from money raised by sponsored roundabouts.

It took Rob three days to complete the work. He has also worked on a number of other carvings throughout the district.

2017

- **May:** A terrorist bombing attack at an Ariana Grande concert in Manchester, England kills 22 people and injures over 140.
- **May:** Emmanuel Macron becomes President of France after defeating far-right candidate Marine Le Pen.
- **June:** Grenfell Tower fire in London kills 72 and injures 70.
- **June:** The queen reaches her sapphire jubilee – 65 years on the throne. The queen and Prince Philip celebrate their platinum wedding anniversary after 70 years of marriage.

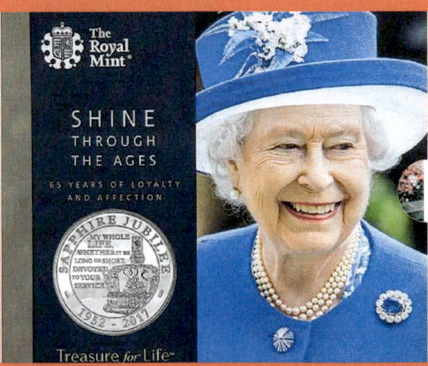

- **July:** Britain's latest Aircraft Carrier, The Queen Elizabeth was launched on 17th July 2014, and comissioned on 7th December 2017.
- **October:** Allegations of sexual abuse against film producer Harvey Weinstein lead to a wave of similar accusations from within Hollywood and other areas of primarily the English-speaking world.
- **November:** Robert Mugabe is ousted from Zimbabwe in a coup d'état.

Best Place to Live in the UK

A study in 2017 found that, yet again, Hart was the best place to live in the whole of the UK. This was the 5th time in 6 years that the district has come out on top. The Halifax study covered factors such as life expectancy, earnings, employment and crime. 97% of locals are in good or fairly good health. Hart enjoys 32.5 hours of sun a week compared to the national average of 29.7. In 2017 the average house price was £419,000.

Fleet Infants becomes Grade II Listed

Fleet Infant School (formely Velmead Infants) was granted Grade II Listed Building Status by Historic England in 2017.

The school was designed by Hopkins and Partners in 1984-1985, and built in 1985-1986 for Hampshire County Council. It was listed for reasons of architectural interest, as an inventive and engaging solution to the design of an infant school by a leading architectural practice, and constructional interest, as a predominantly glazed, light-weight steel frame.

Edenbrook Country Park Opened

Edenbrook Park is a Suitable Alternate Natural Greenspace (SANG) and offers pleasant natural amenities. It is managed by Berkelely Homes group.

The site is placed at the back of the

new Hart leisure centre in Hitches Lane and has a variety of habitats including ponds, wetlands, sprawling meadows and woodland areas with 84 acres of leisure space.

New Hart Leisure Centre Opens

The building of the new Hart Leisure Centre was completed in May 2017. The centre opened on 1 April 2017 and Hart District Council appointed Everyone Active, a management company, to manage the whole site on its behalf. £23 million was invested by Hart District Council in this prestigious new facility located on the edge of Edenbrook Country Park.

2018

- **Feb:** Jacob Zuma resigns as President of South Africa; Cyril Ramaphosa becomes President.
- **April:** Birth of Prince Louis of Cambridge.
- **May:** Prince Harry marries Meghan Markle in St George's Chapel at Windsor Castle.

- **June:** Saudi Arabia allows women to drive.
- **October:** Exiled Washington Post journalist Jamal Khashoggi is assassinated inside the Saudi consulate in Istanbul.
- **November:** Yellow vest movement becomes France's largest sustained period of civil unrest since 1968.
- **November:** Leaders from around the world attend the centennial of the ending of the First World War.

Norma Howard Becomes Oldest UK Woman to Wing-Walk

A 91-year-old retired physiotherapist was thought to have become the UK's oldest female wing-walker. Norma Howard, from Fleet in Hampshire, was strapped to a vintage biplane for the challenge, which raised almost £2,000 for charity Dementia UK. Mrs Howard was attached to the top wing of the aircraft before flying to a height of 500ft (152m).

Elvis Impersonator Honoured

Fleet Lions Club honoured the longest running Elvis Tribute act in the world for his fundraising work.

It was a total surprise for Crondall resident Dave Hurrell when at the end of a Lions club concert, it was announced the Lions were presenting him with the Melvin Jones Fellowship, the highest award within the Lions International movement.

For decades, in his guise as Dale Fontaine, Mr Hurrell had performed his echoes of Elvis show at venues across the area for the benefit of numerous local causes. For the past 25 years, Dale has been a regular at the Lions Fun Fest.

Animal Trail in Fleet

In Summer 2018, Fleet Town Centre became a temporary Safari Park, with statues of wild animals making up a Summer Trail. Life sized zebra, lion, hippo, rhino and a gorilla were dispersed throughout the town and those completing the trail were entered into a competition to win a £100 voucher. The trail was an initiative of the Business Improvement District (BID) to encourage visitors to return to our town.

Fleet and District Beekeepers Association 100 Years Old

Fleet and District Beekeepers Association celebrated its 100 years anniversary with a special talk by a committee member. The group was formed on March 15th 1918 and now has over 200 members and 30 non-bee keeping members in the NE Hampshire area. The society exists "to promote and further the craft and science of beekeeping and to advance the education of the public in the importance of honey bees to the environment".

2019

- **January:** Chang'e 4 becomes the first object to land on the far side of the Moon.
- **January:** The motion to approve the Brexit withdrawal agreement was rejected 202–432. This was the largest defeat on a government motion in history.
- **April:** The Event Horizon Telescope takes the first ever image of a black hole, at the core of galaxy Messier 87.
- **April:** A major fire engulfs Notre-Dame Cathedral in Paris, resulting in the roof and main spire collapsing.

- **May:** Archie Harrison Mountbatten-Windsor is born to the Duke and Duchess of Sussex.
- **July:** Theresa May formally tenders her resignation as Prime Minister to Queen Elizabeth II, and is succeeded by Boris Johnson.
- **September:** Greta Thunberg delivers "How dareyou" speech at the 2019 UN Climate Action Summit.

Historic Steam Train Passing through Fleet.

Flying Scotsman passes through Fleet Station 12 April 2019.

Plaque Unveiled at ex-County Commercial Cars Site

In October 2019 a plaque commemorating the location of the County Commercial Cars factory that closed in 1983, was unveilled in Albert Street.

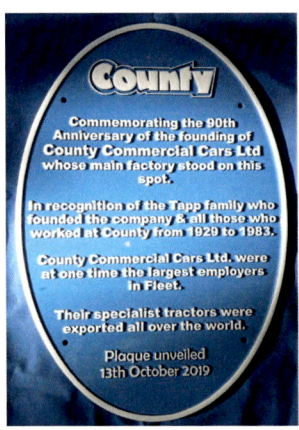

Antiques Road Trip Show comes to Serendipity

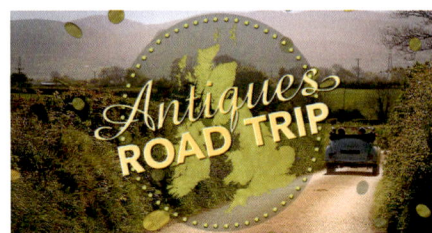

In December 2019, Charlie Ross from The Antiques Road Trip paid a visit to the Serendipity shop in Fleet Rd. He spent a couple of hours looking at a couple of items before finally deciding to buy something. The BBC broadcast the show in Febuary 2020.

Marco George World Record

Marco George from Fleet broke the world record for fastest speed on a motorbike while performing a headstand when he reached a speed of 76 mph. Once he got comfortable in a headstand whilst moving, Marco kept trying to beat that speed as a personal challenge that tested his bottle, strength and skill.

The whole process took three years, from learning to do a headstand to attempting and beating the record.

2020

- **January:** Prince Harry and Meghan quit royal life in Britain and move to the USA.
- **January:** Donald Trump is acquitted by the United States Senate in his first impeachment trial.
- **January:** The United Kingdom formally withdraws from the European Union.
- **March:** The COVID-19 virus spreads from China to the vast majority of the world's inhabited areas, infecting at least 81 million and killing at least 1.8 million people in its first year.
- **March:** A national lockdown takes place due to the coronavirus pandemic. Freedom of movement is restricted and this becomes enforceable in law. Non-essential shops and services close.
- **April:** The Queen gave a rare televised speech to address the coronavirus pandemic. It was watched by around 24 million people.

- **May:** The murder of George Floyd sparks racial justice protests across the United States and the world.
- **November:** Joe Biden is elected President of the USA.

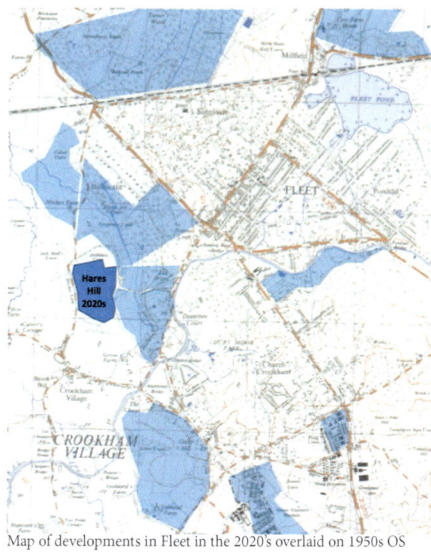

Map of developments in Fleet in the 2020's overlaid on 1950s OS Map. Note previous developments from 1950s to 2010s are shaded in blue

Papa Johns Pizza team wins fastest Pizza makers in the "Pizza Games"

Papa Johns pizza making team were the winners in the 2020 Pizza Games under the category "Fastest Pizza makers in the Country". The team managed to make and cook 10 pizzas in 8 minutes and 53 seconds!

Local girl Kate Ovens becomes social media celeb

Fleet girl Kate Ovens has established a huge social media following through unbelievable eating challenges. So far she has chalked up a 27-inch pizza, 3kg Kebab, 74oz steak, 58oz burger. In June 2020 she added to her toll with a 32oz fish and chips supper.

Night club Moo Moos Becomes Zinc Popworld

Moo Moo nightclub in Upper Street Fleet was converted into a Zinc and Popworld. There was a closing party at the old club on February 1st. The newly refurbished club was re-opened in March 2020, just in time to be closed down because of Covid-19 restrictions. The cost of the update was thought to be around £300,000.

The venue had already undergone two re-brands, initially being called The Warehouse and Jaxx before transforming into Moo Moos in 2015.

Albert Street Social Club Closed

Albert Street Social Club in Albert Street Fleet wasn't able to re-open following the end of Coronavirus restrictions. The club had faced a number of challenges in the previous decade and had been struggling financially as well as with a number of issues relating to its non-optimal acoustic design. The club had served Fleet since the early 70's providing a venue for many private parties and functions, as well as member-only prices and a welcoming atmosphere. Many ex-members will remember bingo, darts, snooker and of course the weekly meat raffle.

2021

- **January:** Supporters of President Donald Trump, gathered after a rally led by him, attack the United States Capitol - one demonstrator was shot.
- **March:** The container ship Ever Given obstructs the Suez Canal for six days, costing an estimated $3.6 billion in global trade.
- **April:** Prince Philip, Queen Elizabeth II's husband, dies aged 99 on April 9th 2021. He was the longest-serving British Consort.

- **June:** Prince Harry and Meghan Markle name their baby daughter Lilibet after Queen Elizabeth.

- **August:** Kabul falls. The war in Afghanistan ends after 20 years following the withdrawal of U.S. and coalition troops.
- **November:** Russia begins a military buildup on the Ukrainian border, warning NATO not to intervene.

Bakers Closing

Bakers hardware shop, the oldest remaining shop on Fleet Road, closed in 2021.

Lions Funfest

Fleet Lions entertained around 500 guests at their annual Funfest event which gave a free day of activities for disabled people and their families and helpers. David Styler, a Fleet Lions member and chairman of the organising team, commented on the event: "It has been a very difficult year for everyone, so we were so pleased to be able to hold the Lions Funfest event this year".

Carla Denyer

Carla Denyer was born and lived her early life in Fleet. In 2021 she was elected national co-leader of the Green Party.

Celebrity Paddle Boarding along Canal

Charley Boorman, former England footballer Wayne Bridge and F1 champion Damon Hill were joined by England rugby star James Haskell and presenter Chloe Madeley in a paddle boarding challenge along the whole length of the Basingstoke canal.

All Saints Church Finally begins Rebuild

The Reverend Mark Hayton announced that permission had finally been granted to rebuild the All Saints Church. Construction work began in the middle of the year and should be complete by early 2023.

Scoop Success

Eco-friendly zero waste shop Scoop, that was located in Reading Road South, moved to a larger store in Fleet Road next to Cafe Amica and Starbucks. The shop was founded by Kate Cottrell less than two years ago. Kate was a primary school teacher for 11 years, but has made the transition to shop-keeper and eco-warrior very successfully. Customers can bring in their own containers or buy them in store to fill with various items including baking, dry foods, toiletries, dried nuts, fruits, seeds and even cleaning products.

Fleet War Memorial is 100 years old

In April 2021 the War Memorial in Gurkha Square reached its 100th anniversary. A short film was made by NRG Digital and the Fleet, Crookham & District Branch of the Royal British Legion to celebrate the rededication of the Memorial and also trace its history. The video is available on Facebook.

2022

- **January: Prince Andrew stops using HRH title and loses military titles.**
- **February: Queen Elizabeth II's Platinum Jubilee, marking 70 years on the British throne.**
- **February: Russia invades Ukraine.**
- **February: Boris Johnson lifts all restriction and tells the country "we must live with Covid".**
- **February: Her Majesty announces that Camilla will be queen.**
- **March: Her Majesty decided to leave Buckingham Palace for good and make a permanent move to Windsor Castle.**
- **May: Inflation in UK reaches 9%.**
- **June: Queen Elizabeth II and the whole country celebrates her Platinum Jubilee.**

Helen Bauer Enjoys Fleet in "small doses"

Local girl Helen Bauer has written and starred in a pilot sitcom, in which she follows the main character returning from Germany to her home town of Fleet, after a stint as an au-pair. Small Doses isn't necessarily kind to Hampshire and describes Fleet as a 'very boring, non-descript town' in the introduction. Bit harsh, but Helen makes clear on her Instagram account "I made a pilot of a sitcom. A sitcom I have had in my head forever. It's set in my hometown of Fleet and I hope you love it and everyone in it is so great and the team who made it happen are literal dream makers".

Zara Tindall at Tweaseldown

Zara Tindall, the Queen's eldest granddaughter rides in March 2022 at the Tweseldown Horse Trials for a day of show jumping, cross country and dressage. In March 2021 she gave birth to son Lucas. Zara won a silver medal at the 2012 London Olympics.

Nazanin Zaghari-Ratcliffe released

Richard Ratcliffe, originally from Fleet, saw his wife Nazanin Zaghari-Ratcliffe finally released from wrongful imprisonment in Iran.

Richard had waged a high-profile campaign to keep Nazanin at the forefront of people minds throughtout her ordeal, including a hunger strike in 2021. Throughout the campaign Richard's parents, living in Fleet, had kept a prominent poster stating "Free Nazanin, Bring our Girls Back".

Fleet Girl Charlotte Harris in Pair who Beat World Record Rowing the Atlantic

Jessica Oliver, 29, and Charlotte Harris, 30, cruised 3,000 miles to victory in the Atlantic challenge, on the way breaking the world record for the fastest female pair to cross the Atlantic, ahead of 35 other teams from all over the world. The friends battled 30ft waves, sleep deprivation, hallucinations, blisters, sharks, capsizing and even a mid-ocean collision in their boat Cosimo. They finished five days ahead of their nearest rivals in the pairs category of the Talisker Whisky Atlantic Challenge when they reached Antigua on January 26. They also wiped the same number of days off the previous female pairs' world record in a time of 45 days, seven hours and 25 minutes. The two British women had no previous rowing experience before the event!

Geoff Baker awarded "Freedom of the Town"

Geoff Baker, owner of Baker's Hardware Store in Fleet, was given the highest honour that can be bestowed upon a resident of Fleet when he was awarded the "Freedom of the Town" on 22nd March 2022. The citation on the award reads "for the valuable and devoted public services rendered to the residents of Fleet. During your time you have served the Community of Fleet as friend of Fleet Hospital, Fleet Rotary and contributed time and efforts to the Remembrance Sunday and the War Memorial. In recognition of the longstanding and eminent service which you have rendered to the community of Fleet. We loudly applaud your valuable and sterling service whilst thanking you most sincerely."

2022
Thu 2 June

Lantern Parade

Over 400 people from the All Saints C of E Junior School community joined together and paraded carrying home-made lanterns. The parade began at Fleet Town Football club and processed into Calthorpe Park. The effect was stunning. The children formed a dramatic line a safe distance from the beacon.

Beacon Lighting

At 9.45pm precisely, at a ceremony at Windsor Castle, the Queen queen was presented with a "Commonwealth of Nations Globe" which she pressed to trigger the start of beacon lighting across the UK. At Buckingham Palace, Prince William and others watching on as the Tree of Trees sculpture was illuminated following the Queen's initiation in Windsor. In Fleet, around 4,000 people in Calthorpe Park witnessed Fleet's beacon be lit by our first Honorary Freeman, Geoff Baker. Around 3,000 beacons were simultaneously lit across the UK.

Beacon lighting is a traditional element of British royal celebrations that began as a way for people far from London to take part in festivities.

Fireworks

Following the Beacon lighting, the crowd at Calthorpe Park were treated to a Fireworks display. The spectacular display rounded off the first day of the 4-days of celebrations that Fleet had planned.

2022
Fri 3 June

Fleet 30 mile Cycling Event

Local scouts planned and organised two cycle rides on Day Two of the Jubilee celebrations. The 30-mile ride saw cyclists setting off from Calthorpe Park in groups of around 8-10 riders at one-minute intervals from 9 am. The route took them out through Hartley Wintney, Tunworth and right out to Old Basing, before bringing them back through Upton Grey to finish at Calthorpe Park. Over 120 cyclists took part in the event, each doing their very best to get round in good time. The weather was perfect, the route was clearly signed and rescue crews had to respond to only two technical mishaps. Finishers were eligible to buy a Platinum Jubilee commemorative medallion bearing the official Jubilee crown logo and the scout logo.

Family 10 mile Bike Ride

The second ride organised by the scout team was a more sedate 10-mile route which was perfect for families and beginners. The route allowed families to enjoy great views of our local countryside and to explore local roads without the heavy traffic. Over 180 adults and children set off in waves of around 12 from 10 am and had a perfect start to Day 2 of the celebrations. Most riders returned to Calthorpe Park at around midday, to find the previously empty park had been transformed into a wonderland of diverse activities.

Activity Stalls

Local community organisations turned out in strength to allow all ages to enjoy activities throughout the Friday afternoon. Over 50 stands and stalls were available, offering activities ranging from the highly physical like "Hang tough", dancing-based Clubbercise, and two giant inflatable assault courses, to the more skilful activities of Archery, Tomahawk throwing, inflatable football darts, football speed shooting and a coconut shy. Less skilful events, but no less fun for all the family, were lucky dips, tombolas, operation, buzzy wires and splat the rat. Our local vicar even allowed all and sundry to pelt him with wet sponges

and fire water guns at him.

All-in-all the afternoon was a delight with superb weather, great music from Frimley Park Radio and a wonderful atmosphere. Large queues for refreshments and food demonstrated just how well attended the event was.

Dog Show

Several local dog owners and businesses clubbed together to make sure our four-legged friends could also join in with the celebrations too. Competitions were held for the Cutest Puppy, the Golden Oldie, Best Rescue Dog, Most Fabulous Fella, Loveliest Lady and the Best Dog at doing tricks. Keeping with the dog theme, prize-winners received not only a rosette but also a 'pup cake'.

Basingstoke Canal Rally

From midday on Friday 3rd, the Jubilee committee organised a very successful boat rally. Attracting boats, canoes, kayaks and paddleboards the event was so well attended that many people who wished to visit couldn't do so because of queues and crowds. The Fox and Hounds Public House laid on a BBQ and provided live music to while away the afternoon. Sea Scouts also gave a performance of their skills which was entertaining and amusing to those fortunate to find a space along the canal bank.

Community Quiz

On the evening of Friday 3rd, the Jubilee committee held a sell-out Community Jubilee Quiz at The Key Centre, Elvetham Heath. 17 teams tackled eight Jubilee-themed question rounds including Royal trivia, Red, White and Blue pop groups and a picture round identifying famous 70-year-olds. Great fun was had by all and the eventual winning team "I Can't See to Write" triumphed by three points over second-place "Yateley Young 'Uns". A magnificent £1,700 was raised, which will be used to support former Service personnel who find themselves in need.

2022
Sat 4 June

7 Decades of Motoring Procession

Not many people realise, but Fleet is home to one of the most successful classic car storage businesses in Europe! So, when the Jubilee committee asked if it would be possible to organise a procession of the best cars from each decade of the Queens reign, Universal Classic Cars rose to the challenge. Their appeal to local classic car owners resulted in a phenomenal response – forcing the organisers to select only the very finest examples from all the applicants. Cars that made the cut were really very special. Millions of pounds worth of beautiful and iconic cars processed along Fleet Road making their way eventually to a static display in Calthorpe Park.

One logistical challenge was ensuring that cars passing the cricket match at the park's entrance were not damaged by a ball to the bodywork. A stop/go system ensured no casualties and the procession was a tremendous success. Two County tractors, originally built in Fleet, and two Fire Engines completed the procession.

Jubilee Parade

Immediately behind the car procession came the Sandhurst and District Corps of Drums leading a parade of local organisations. The parade, organised by a local scout leader, included contingents from the Army Cadets, the Royal British Legion and veterans, local councillors, Boys and Girls Brigades, Fleet Pond Society, the WI and U3A. The second portion of the parade was led by the 14th Eastleigh Scout and Guide Band (The Spitfires) and included Rainbows, Brownies and Guides, Squirrels, Beavers, Cubs and Scouts and Explorers, Hart Road Runners, the Rotary and Heatherside School and the "Rotary express". The tremendous turnout of over 1000 participants was watched and applauded by over 4000 spectators along Fleet Road who then followed the parade down to Calthorpe Park. Never has Fleet been so filled with flags, uniforms, style, and pride in Her Majesty.

Salute from Deputy Lieutenant of Hampshire

Once the Jubilee Parade had reached Calthorpe Park, accompanied by crowds that had lined the

parade route, the assembled groups were welcomed by Chairman of Fleet Town Council, Cllr Bob Schofield who introduced the Deputy Lieutenant of Hampshire, Mark Thislethwayte, who was present as the monarch's representative. The Deputy Lieutenant praised the work of Jubilee events committee led by Sue Tilley to deliver the four-day Jubilee extravaganza and admired the parade's size, variety, colour and music as a "great local display".

Following a rousing chorus of the National Anthem, Parade Organiser David Millen led three cheers for the Queen. The parade and crowds slowly dispersed to enjoy viewing the parked-up classic cars, community stalls or just sitting in the park enjoying a sunny Saturday. Some 8,000-10,000 people were estimated to be in Calthorpe Park at the end of the parade, showing great community participation and spirit. The throng of happy revellers made all the planning and organising worth the effort and showed Fleet at it's best.

Cabaret and Supper at the Harlington

The Jubilee committee hosted a Cabaret and Celebration Supper with internationally acclaimed celebrity entertainer Colin Roy who had the audience on their feet dancing the night away to great swing, soul and Motown tunes. Supper was a fine selection of cheeses, continental meats and desserts. Of course, a glass of bubbles was on hand to toast the Queen. A superb night's entertainment flawlessly delivered by a team of ladies who work tirelessly for the community.

2022
Sun 5 June

Fun Run

The scout team were at it again on Sunday, organising two running events in Calthorpe Park. Almost 20 children aged 3 to 7 completed a width of the park to huge encouragement from the 120 runners lined up for their 5km Fun Run. They fully earned their Platinum Jubilee Medallions. The run took them on a scenic route around parks, a bridle way, Edenbrook Country Park and Baker Way and was a great opportunity to burn off some calories before inevitably putting them back on during the Street Party.

Act of Worship Family Service

The weather forecast for Sunday, even the night before, was for constant heavy rain. For the town's Christians that might have dampened proceedings but it would have ruined the Street Party that was to follow. Clearly, prayers were answered as the rain held off all day without even a shower until the heavens opened at 6 PM which effectively ended the day.

The Act of Worship was an inter-denominational event involving all local Churches that took over Gurkha Square and the Stage and Sound systems from 9.45 to 11.15. The service enjoyed a huge congregation who filled the square with hearty singing and the message focused on celebrating the Queen's life combining this with a celebration of the Day of Pentecost, which fell on that Sunday.

Street Party

The street party was due to open at midday but as soon as stalls were up, the hungry crowds descended. A wide variety of foods and beverages were represented and there was something for every taste. Tables and benches were placed in all the Fleet Road parking bays, encouraging revellers to sit and enjoy their food, soak up the atmosphere and enjoy the music. Sunday marked a superb culmination of four days of well-organised, varied, safe and enthralling activities. The voluntary and community groups that formed Fleet Jubilee Committee five months earlier were rightly pleased with how incredibly well the whole weekend had gone. The people of Fleet celebrated in style.

Gurkha Square Music Bands

After the service, the stage was filled by Shuffle Tunes who opened the afternoon's Live Entertainment. They were followed by Get Plucky, DJ Chunkster, John Galantini, Phil Rees, Modern Jive Kings and St. P&J Church Jazz Band.

Using a high-tech speaker system, the live music from Gurkha Square was relayed along the Fleet Road and across to the Views, which became a picnic venue. Modern Jive Kings from Mytchett gave a lesson to all and had scores of people dancing superbly to modern tunes. Several local bands and DJs performed on stage throughout the duration of the street party, providing great entertainment for all. The final act of the evening, the Ultimate Party Band, was, unfortunately, rained-off at the very end of the evening.

Aknowledgements:

This book is a compilation of a Poster Trail that chronicled 70 years of history in Fleet and Crookham, while Queen Elizabeth II has been reigning on the throne of the United Kingdom. It also includes artistic contributions from many local school children, who have designed artworks to celebrate the Queen's Platinum Jubilee and her central role in British life.

The programme includes photographs and an account of the activities that were carried out as part of the Jubilee celebrations between Thursday 2nd June and Sunday 5th June.

It is published as a souvenir of the events associated with celebrating the Queens Platinum Jubilee, and the period of local history throught which she has reigned.

The Platinum Jubilee Committee would like to acknowledge the help that has been provided by the Fleet and Crookham Local History Group, and particularly Phylis Ralton, in the research and preparation of information contained in the historical aspects of the posters and the provision of illustrative photographs.

The Platinum Jubilee Committee would also like to acknowledge the materials sourced from forFleetsSake.co.uk.

Finally, the Platinum Jubilee Committee would also like to thank and acknowledge Aldershot, Farnham and Fleet Camera Club, and local photographer Kevin Whibley of Captured Moment and Nigel Box for the provision of the photographs that were used to chronicle the events of the Jubilee celebrations.

1952
Housing Crisis FCLHG 1952.09.003
Fleet Cycle Speedway – From Facebook
All other Pictures Creative Commons License (CCL)

1953
Carnival Programme – ForFleetsSake.co.uk
Carnival – ForFleetsSake.co.uk
Carnival Parade – From Facebook
Clarence Road Street Party – From Facebook
Fleet Town FC Insignia – From FTFC
GUS Cartoonist – From FCLHG
All other Pictures CCL

1954
Fleet Cycle Speedway Team – From Facebook
Peter Driver Images – Copyright Alan Driver
GCGS – Church Crookham Garden Society
Pantomime – From Facebook
All other Pictures CCL

1955
Stevens Bros – From Facebook
St. Nicks Pupils – From Facebook
Gally Hill Road – From Facebook
Fleet Road – From Facebook
All other Pictures CCL

1956
Carnival Queen – ForFleetsSake.co.uk
Carnival Programme – ForFleetsSake.co.uk
Crookham Memorial Hall – From Facebook
Freddie Mills - FCLHG 2018.124.030.001
Queen Mother at QE Barracks – From Facebook
All other Pictures CCL

1957
NGTE Aerial View – From Facebook
Fleet Cinema – From Facebook
All other Pictures CCL

1958
Catholic Church – Ros Einchcomb
Tweseldown – Tweseldown.co.uk
All other Pictures CCL

1959
Crookham Social Club – From Facebook
North Hants Tyres – From Facebook
Street Scenes – From Facebook
All other Pictures CCL

1960
Fleet and Crookham Athletic Club – fleetandcrookhamac.club
Cricket Club – ForFleetsSake.co.uk
Lido – From Facebook
All other Pictures CCL

1961
Rotary Insignia – rotary-ribi.org
Townswomen's Guild – Patricia Jackson
Aircraft Crash – MoD Accident investigation
Home Decorating – From Facebook
All other Pictures CCL

1962
Ray Oldham – Ray Oldham
Fleet Road – From Facebook
All other Pictures CCL

1963
Mummers - FCLHG 2019.040.206
County Commercial Tractor Models and Photos –
Simon Fenwick
All other Pictures CCL

1964
Churches – Ros Einchcomb
Street Scenes – From Facebook
All other Pictures CCL

1965
Church Crookham Junior School – crookham-jun.hants.sch.uk
Churches – Ros Einchcomb
Engine Test Cell – Rolls Royce
Street Scenes – From Facebook
All other Pictures CCL

1966
Juliet Aubrey – Juliet Aubrey
Wiggs Pool – Fleet & Odiham Observer
Fleet Lido – Forfleetssake.co.uk
Fleet Language Circle – fleetlanguagecircle.org.uk
Mark Hicks – Basingstoke Canal Society and Hicks family
All other Pictures CCL

1967
Fleet Lido – Forfleetssake.co.uk
Church Crookham Players – churchcrookhamplayers.org.uk
Scouts Church Parade – Forfleetssake.co.uk
Eriva Dene School – From Facebook
All other Pictures CCL

1968
Police Station – Forfleetssake.co.uk
Raquel Cassidy – Raquel Cassidy
County Commercial – County Commercial Cars

Weslyan Church – From Facebook
All other Pictures CCL

1969
All Saints School – From Facebook
Fleet Railway – From Wikipedia Common
Heatherside – From Facebook
All other Pictures CCL

1970
Keith Monks – Keith Monks Audio
Elvetham Estate – elvetham.co.uk
All other Pictures CCL

1971
Scout Hut – 22nd Odiham Scouts
Calthorpe Park School – FCLHG 2009.026.02
All other Pictures CCL

1972
Fleet 10K – Fleet and Crookham Athletic Club
Peter Driver Sports Centre – From Facebook
Methodist Church – Ros Einchcomb
Tavistock Infants – tavistockinfants.co.uk
Hart District Council – hart.gov.uk
All other Pictures CCL

1973
Girl Guides – Girl Guide Association
Fleet Services – Google Mapping
War Memorial – Royal British Legion
All other Pictures CCL

1974
Hart District Council – hart.gov.uk
Chernocke House – From Facebook
Pitch & Put Ticket – From Facebook
Views from 1970s -From Facebook
All other Pictures CCL

1975
Hart Male Voice Choir – Hart Male Voice Choir
Fleet Street Scenes – From Facebook
All other Pictures CCL

1976
The Gulshan – The Gulshan Fleet
Fleet Pond Society – Fleet Pond Society
Fleet Pond – Calendar views of Fleet
Trefoil – Girl Guide Association
All other Pictures CCL

1977
Carnival Cover – Forfleetssake.co.uk
Street Party – From Facebook
Canal Refurbishment – Basingstoke Canal Society

Redifelds – Redifelds Garden Centre
All other Pictures CCL

1978
Queen with Gurkhas – FCLHG 2019.066.02
Queen with Gurkhas – FCLHG 2019.066.01
Queen with Gurkhas – From Facebook
All other Pictures CCL

1979
Carnival Bridge – FCLHG 2018.130.021
Street Scenes – From Facebook
All other Pictures CCL

1980
Bakers & Street Views – From Facebook
Heatherside Infants – From Google Street View
All other Pictures CCL

1981
Church Army Anchorage Home – FCLHG 2010.105.122
Royal Train – FCLHG 2016.153.113.39
All other Pictures CCL

1982
Velmead School – From Facebook
OASIS – From Google Street View
Fleet Half Marathon – From Facebook
Falklands Gurkha Parade – From Facebook
All other Pictures CCL

1983
Guides HQ – Fleet Guides
Bible Bookshop/ LivingStones – LivingStones Christian Centre
Leivgnen/ Crookham Village – Levignen/ Crookham village twinning group
All other Pictures CCL

1984
KFC Logo – KFC
Carnival Programme – Forfleetssake.co.uk
Carnival Photos – From Facebook
John Pinkerton & Canal Dredging – Basingstoke Canal Society
All other Pictures CCL

1985
War memorial – Royal British Legion, Fleet Branch
Fleet and Crookham Local History Group – fchlg.org.uk
Street scene – From Faceebook
All other Pictures CCL

1986
Half Marathon – Forfleetssake.co.uk
Accessible Boating – accessibleboating.org.uk
Fleet Infants – From Facebook
Boys Brigade Logo – Boys Brigade
All other Pictures CCL

1987
Carnival Programme – Forfleetssake.co.uk
Churches – Ros Einchcomb
All other Pictures CCL

1988
Technograph and Telegraph – FCLHG 2009.052.034.01
RAE Insignia – Qinetiq plc
Fleet Cycling – fleetcycling.org.uk
All other Pictures CCL

1989
Pearsons auction house – From Facebook
Probus Logo – Probus International
Road Signs – From Google Street View
All other Pictures CCL

1990
County Commercial Images – County Commercial Cars
Hart Road Runners Logo – hartroadrunners.co.uk
All other Pictures CCL

1991
SD-Scicon – HP
Hart Leisure – Hart District Council
Fleet Rugby Club – aldershotandfleetrugby.com
Opening of Hart Centre – FCLHG 2009.052.050.01
Opening of Hart Centre – FCLHG 2009.052.051.01
Canal Reopening – Basingstoke Canal Society
All other Pictures CCL

1992
Motorway Junction – Google Street View
Dakotas – Forfleetssake.co.uk
Picture by Mabel Wickham – Estate of Mabel Wickham
Velmead Community Centre – Crookham Village Parish Council
All other Pictures CCL

1993
Cana Dredging – Basingstoke Canal Authority
Benson House – Forfleetssake.co.uk

Hart Shopping Centre – Google Street View
Chadney Bulgin – Chadney Bulgin Ltd
All other Pictures CCL

1994
Velmead Farm – From Facebook
Harlington – Fleet Town Council
U3a logo – u3a
All other Pictures CCL

1995
VE Day Day – Forfleetssake.co.uk
Fleet Carnival – Forfleetssake.co.uk
NGTE – Reddit NGTE Pyestock
All other Pictures CCL

1996
St. Nicks School – From Facebook
Eagle Radio – Forfleetssake.co.uk
Emporium - FCLHG 2018.090
Clock – FCLHG 2020.032.02
All other Pictures CCL

1997
Fleet Spurs Logo – Fleet Spurs
Fleet Hospital – From Facebook
Harwoods – Forfleetssake.co.uk
All other Pictures CCL

1998
Lunns/ International Stores/ Prince Arthur – From Facebook
Fleet Choral Society - Fleet Choral Society
All other Pictures CCL

1999
Rose Farm Dairy – From Facebook
Fleet and Crookham in Bloom – Fleet and Crookham in Bloom
Royal British Legion poster – Royal British Legion
Brownies – Brownies association
All other Pictures CCL

2000
Gurkhas Parade – FCLHG 2000.173.11f
Gurkhas Parade – FCLHG 2000.174.03f
CV Library – BBC
Elvetham Heath – FCLHG 2000.177.004.001
Fleet Coaches – From Facebook
Shots Nightclub – From Facebook
All other Pictures CCL

2001
All other Pictures CCL

Fleet Medical Centre – Fleet News and Mail
Fleet Town Girls – Fleet Town Football Club
Fleet Motor Club – Fleet Motor club

2002
Christmas Tree – St. Philip and St. James Church
Heron on the Lake – Heron on the Lake
Bryant Homes – FCLHG 2022.011.001
All other Pictures CCL

2003
URC Church – Ros Einchcomb
Graeme Pullen – Graeme Pullen
Derek Hayes – Hayes family
Fleet Pond society – Fleet Pond society
Christmas Festival – Fleet Town Festival committe
All other Pictures CCL

2004
Helen Reeves – BBC
North Hants Logo – North Hants Golf Club
Morrisons – Morrisons
Crookham Infants – Crookham Infants
Justin Rose - Wikipedia
All other Pictures CCL

2005
Propaganda – From Facebook
Skatepark – Hart District Council
Footbridge – Google Street View
Vicki Hansfords – InsideTheGames
All other Pictures CCL

2006
PortBeagle Shark – Graeme Pullen
Neil Etheridge – Wikipedia
Church on the Heath – Church on the Heath
All other Pictures CCL

2007
Fleet Angels – Fleet Angels
Velmead Common – From Facebook
Fleet Buzz – From Facebook
Pondtail Post Office – From Facebook
All other Pictures CCL

2008
Local History Group Grant – FCHLG 2009.107.2.038
Bakers – Local Data Company
Street Signs – Google Street View
Avondale Logo – Avondale Tennis Club
All other Pictures CCL

2009
Dean and Alison – Sky News
Remembrance Parade – Royal British Legion
Lions Community Store – Fleet Lions
Fleet News and Mail – Fleet News and Mail
Snowy Fleet – From Facebook
All other Pictures CCL

2010
Wrights Bakery – FCLHG 2017.113.026.Wrights
Exchequer Pub – From Facebook
Fleet Town Council Logo – Fleet Town Council
Alan Hope - Wikipedia
All other Pictures CCL

2011
Phyllis Tuckwells re-opening – Phyllis Tuckwell
Ancells Play Area – Fleet Town Council
Fleet Phoenix Logo – Fleet Phoenix
Hart Foodbank Logo – Hart Foodbank
Redfields – Blue Diamond
All other Pictures CCL

2012
Lucy Shuker – Wikipedia
Fleet Jazz Club Logo – Fleet Jazz Club
Haifax Logo – Halifax
Ken Heanes - From Facebook
All other Pictures CCL

2013
Guides Hall – Girl Guides Association
Justin Rose - Denver post
Beca Lye-Pirkis – BBC Bake Off
Fleet Food Festival Logo – Fleet Lions
John Pinkerton 2 – Basingstoke Canal society
All other Pictures CCL

2014
Police Station – Forfleetssake.co.uk
Isobel Pooley – Wikipedia
Tweseldown Infant School – Tweseldown Infant School
Fleet Station – From Facebook
All other Pictures CCL

2015
Archaeology – Thames Valley Archaeological services.
Ant and Dec – Antanddec.com
Fleet Town Football Club Logo – Fleet Town Football Club
All Saints Church – All Saints Church
All other Pictures CCL

2016
Santa Sleigh – Forfleetssake
Fireball – UK Meteor network
Chainsaw Carving – Hart and Fleet Town Councils
All other Pictures CCL

2017
Fleet Infants – Fleet Infant School/ Hopkins and Partners
Hart Leisure Centre – Hart District Council
Edenbrook map – Hart District Council
All other Pictures CCL

2018
Norma Howard – Dementia UK
Animal Trail – Fleet BID
Fleet Bee Keepers – Fleet Bee Keepers
Elvis Impersonator – Fleet News and Mail
All other Pictures CCL

2019
Flying Scotsman Fleet – Fleet News and Mail
County Commercial Plaque – Simon Fenwick
Antiques Road Trip - BBC
Marco George – Marco George
All other Pictures CCL

2020
Papa Johns – Papa Johns Pizza
Kate Ovens – LAD Bible
Zinc Popworld - Stonegate
Albert Street Social Club – Google Street View
All other Pictures CCL

2021
Bakers – W.C. Baker
Carla Denyer – Wikipedia
Scoop – Fleet Scoop
Paddle Boarding – Movember Charity
War memorial – Royal British Legion
All other Pictures CCL

2022
Helen Bauer – BBC
Zara Tindall – Tweseldown Race Course
Geoff Baker – Captured Moment
Charlotte Harris – Talisker Whiskey
All other Pictures CCL

Thurs 2nd June (from top to bottom by column)
Beacon and Moon – Copyright Micheal Carrington AFFC
3-person family – Copyright Micheal Carrington AFFC
Child with lantern – Copyright Micheal Carrington AFFC
2-person family – Copyright Micheal Carrington AFFC
Child with lantern – Copyright Micheal Carrington AFFC
Procession with lanterns – Copyright Micheal Carrington AFFC
Family with flags and lanterns – Copyright Micheal Carrington AFFC
Lanterns in hands – Copyright Micheal Carrington AFFC
Lantern being lit – Copyright Ana Peiro, AFFC
Fireworks 1 – Copyright Ana Peiro, AFFC
Fireworks 2 – Copyright Ana Peiro, AFFC
Fireworks 3 – Copyright Ana Peiro, AFFC
Fireworks 4 – Copyright Ana Peiro, AFFC

Friday 3rd June (from top to bottom by column)
Canal Rally – Copyright Captured Moment
Cyclists on field – Copyright Micheal Carrington AFFC
Tandem cyclists – Copyright Micheal Carrington AFFC
Cyclist with dog – Copyright Micheal Carrington AFFC
Coconut Shy – Copyright Captured Moment
Two girl cyclists - - Copyright Micheal Carrington AFFC
Child with pull-along bike – Copyright Micheal Carrington AFFC
Dog in costume – Copyright Captured Moment
Vicar getting soaked – Copyright Captured Moment
Dog agility – Copyright Captured Moment

Saturday 4th June (from top to bottom by column)
MG car – Copyright Nigel Box
RBL parade - Copyright Micheal Carrington AFFC
Squirrels - Copyright Nigel Box
XGW 344 Car - Copyright Nigel Box
Cadets – Copyright Nigel Box
Beavers - Copyright Nigel Box
Brownies - Copyright Nigel Box
Morris Minor - Copyright Micheal Carrington AFFC
County Tractors - Copyright Ana Peiro, AFFC
Deputy Lieutenant - Copyright Micheal Carrington AFFC

Sunday 5th June (from top to bottom by column)
Street Party Crowd - Copyright Micheal Carrington AFFC
Family with union flags & colour - Copyright Micheal Carrington AFFC
Family with faces painted - Magda Pascoe
Young women outside Pizza Express – Copyright Heather Bailey
Lady with Union Flag top and trimmings - Copyright Micheal Carrington AFFC
Stilt walker – Magda Pascoe
Guitar player – Copyright Captured Moment
Fun run - Copyright Micheal Carrington AFFC
Act of Worship 1 - Copyright Micheal Carrington AFFC
Act of Worship 2 - Copyright Micheal Carrington AFFC
Ukele Band - Copyright Micheal Carrington AFFC

JUBILEE FUN FOR EVERYONE!
With thanks to our Sponsors and Supporters

www.fleetplatinumjubilee.co.uk

www.ingramcontent.com/pod-product-compliance
Lightning Source LLC
Chambersburg PA
CBRC091206070526
44584CB00009B/337